CHINESE RUGS

CHINESE RUGS
A Buyer's Guide

Lee Allane

With 94 illustrations, 42 in color

Thames and Hudson

Acknowledgments

I would like to express my gratitude to Hans Christensen, Paul Garrod, Richard Lee, Alain Rouveure, Iain Scott-Stewart and Sam Wennek for their considerable help, and advice on Chinese, Nepalese/Tibetan and other Far Eastern rugs. Thanks are also due to Phuntsog Wangyal, for aiding my understanding of Tibetan culture and Buddhism, and to Meredith Churchill (S.C.M., Lic. Ac., M.T.A.S.) for allowing me the benefit of her expertise on Chinese medicine and other aspects of Chinese culture. A very special debt of gratitude must also be extended to Andrew Daws and Dick Scott-Stewart for their hard work and diligence in producing the superb illustrations and photographs used in this book. And finally, my thanks to Glynis Bell for her invaluable assistance in helping me to unravel the geographical and cultural complexities of the Himalayas and northern India.

I must also acknowledge the courtesy and cooperation of Rippon Boswell Ltd, L. Kelati Ltd, and Alain Rouveure (Cross Cottage Galleries) in supplying the majority of rugs contained in this book. Additional rugs were supplied by OCM (London) Ltd, and from the private collection of Nash Dan. I would also like to thank Messrs Chandni Chowk and Himalayan Kingdoms Ltd for their valuable assistance and advice.

I am especially grateful to Caroline Palmer for her patience, good humour and invaluable assistance in the preparation of the text.

The sources of the colour plates are as follows: Dick Scott-Stewart 1–8, 11–12, 14, 16–20, 23–30, 32, 36–7, 39–42; Alain Rouveure 31, 33–5, 38; OCM (London) Ltd 9–10, 13–15, 21–2.

Line drawings by Andrew Daws
Original photography by Dick Scott-Stewart

First published in the United States of America in 1993 by Thames and Hudson Inc., 500 Fifth Avenue, New York, New York 10110

Library of Congress Catalog Card Number 92-80332

Printed and bound in Singapore

Contents

How to use this book

You may find the range of Chinese and Nepalese-Tibetan rugs on offer in the dealer's showroom or department store quite overwhelming, particularly as rugs that look almost identical may be on sale at vastly different prices. *Chinese Rugs: A Buyer's Guide* has been systematically organized to answer all your immediate questions, as well as to provide you with an indispensable long-term source of reference.

IF YOU ARE A COMPLETE BEGINNER, turn to Chapter I, which tells you what Chinese rugs are and explains which countries fall under the *Chinese sphere of influence*. Here you will find a clear explanation of *essential rug-making terms* and useful background information on the *Chinese language*. Chapter II explains *how rugs are made*, and how the different *techniques, tools and materials* affect the quality and character of a particular rug.

Armed with this background knowledge of the subject, you will now feel confident enough to contemplate **BUYING A RUG**. Chapter III will help you to choose *the right rug at the right price*. It explains how to avoid the pitfalls of paying too much, or buying something that is unsuitable for your needs. You will learn how to recognize particular rug types and ranges, and how to assess *quality and value for money*. There is an invaluable guide to the *relative prices* of the different rug ranges, together with hints on *where and when to buy*, and advice on how to care for your rug.

IF YOU WANT TO KNOW MORE about a rug you already own, or to develop your interest in the subject, Chapter IV puts your rug into its **CULTURAL CONTEXT**, providing a brief history of China and the Chinese people. It also provides a fascinating insight into **CHINESE BELIEFS** and explores the way these permeate every aspect of Chinese culture and life. This theme is continued in Chapter V, which explains the origin and symbolic meanings of *design schemes and motifs*, and the hidden mysticism that underpins nearly all Chinese designs.

For the more serious student, Chapter VI provides information on **OLD AND ANTIQUE RUGS** from China and the Chinese sphere of influence. It covers the development of rug-making in each individual country and region, as well as their *traditional weaving groups*. Chapter VII is devoted to **CONTEMPORARY RUGS**. It contains a comprehensive guide to the *current ranges* of rugs available from China, Nepal and other parts of the Far East. There are descriptions of quality, design repertoire, colour schemes and grades, which will enable you to identify the majority of *Chinese* rugs on the market today.

Clear cross-references and headings, supplemented by a thorough index, allow you to move easily through the text, referring to the explanatory *maps* and *line drawings*. *Colour plates* – chosen to illustrate designs or types of rug typical of those that are currently available – offer instant visual examples to supplement the explanations in the text.

This book will remain a valuable source of **PERMANENT REFERENCE**, whether in the store or museum, at auction, college or at home.

CHAPTER I

Defining a Chinese rug

Any rug made in China could legitimately be described as a Chinese rug, but in practice this term is normally only used in reference to 'hand-knotted' or 'hand-woven' rugs. When applied to contemporary rugs, it defines items produced within the national boundaries of modern China. However, when referring to old and antique items, it is often employed in a wider context to describe rugs with a specific 'Chinese' style and character. National borders have changed dramatically over the centuries, and China now occupies a vastly different geographical area to the one it did when many of the older rugs still on the market were actually made. Consequently, a rug produced in Manchuria during the 18th century, for example, would properly be described as Manchurian; but, in practice, dealers will often use the general definition 'Chinese' to describe any rug with Chinese characteristics, even if its country of origin was not part of China when the rug was made.

The situation is further complicated by the fact that China now produces numerous rugs based on Persian and other designs, which, although Chinese in origin, are not 'Chinese' in character. Also, since its annexation in 1950 Tibet, which has its own distinctive rug-making tradition, no longer produces Tibetan rugs (although 'Tibetan-style' rugs are now made in other parts of China). Contemporary Tibetan rugs are produced exclusively by Tibetan refugees in Nepal, India and other parts of the Far East.

In summary, we can say that there are three broad definitions of a Chinese rug. In the case of contemporary items (i.e. rugs made in the last forty to fifty years), the term is used to describe any handmade rug produced in China, regardless of its style or appearance, or whether it has been based on a traditional Chinese, Persian, Turkoman or other oriental rug design. Second, in the context of older rugs, it may be applied to items produced in territories that are now within China, but were independent countries at the time the rugs were made. And third, it is often employed as a general description of rugs with an overall 'Chinese' character and style.

Clarifying terms In order to avoid confusion, in subsequent sections of this book the word 'Chinese' will be written in standard script when referring to rugs produced within the national boundaries of China, and in italic, as '*Chinese*', whenever it is used in a wider context to describe a general style of rug. The same system will be used for rugs from other producing countries and regions: i.e. Persian and Turkoman, for example, when describing rugs of these origins, and *Persian* and *Turkoman* when referring to rugs made in these styles.

Cloud meander border (Yuan Dynasty)

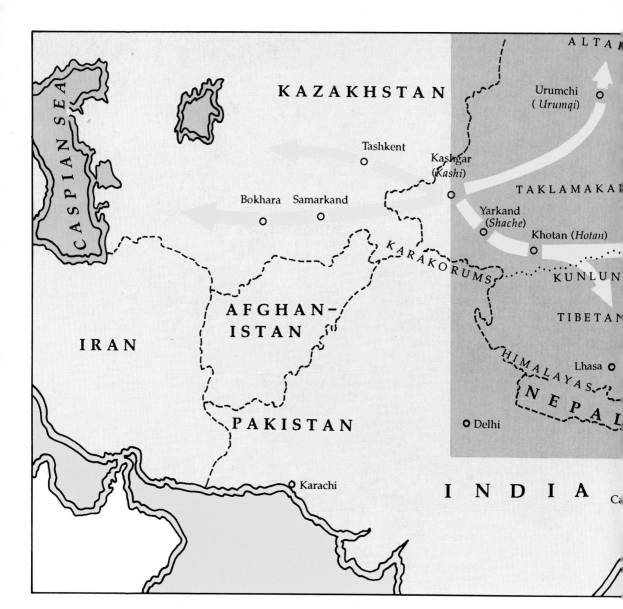

The Chinese sphere of influence

Anyone looking at Chinese, Tibetan, Mongolian or East Turkestan rugs cannot avoid noticing both their similarities to each other and their contrast with Persian and other predominantly 'Islamic' rugs. The symbolism, colouring and general character of *Chinese* rugs in many ways reflect the wider cultural, religious and ethnic division between the Middle East and southern Asia, and the Far East. In the context of rug-making, Asia can be divided into two distinct, though closely interconnected, spheres of influence: the *Persian/Islamic*

and the *Chinese*. If a line were drawn running northwards and eastwards from the northwestern tip of India, all the countries to the west and south of that line (India, Pakistan, Afghanistan, Iran etc.) could be said to fall under the *Persian/Islamic* sphere of influence, and all those to the east and north (Tibet, Mongolia, China etc.) under the *Chinese*.

The pivotal region, in both geographical and rug-making terms, is the vast area of Central Asia known traditionally as Turkestan, which lay between Siberia in the

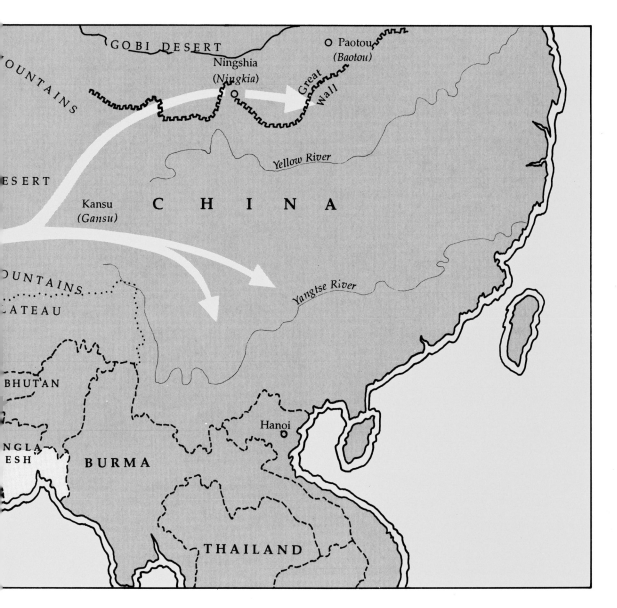

The Chinese sphere of influence and the Silk Route

north and Tibet, India, Afghanistan and Iran in the south. This arid and inhospitable territory covered an area of several million square miles and was largely inhabited by nomadic and semi-nodamic peoples of general Turkic (Turkoman) origin, including Uighur, Tadzhik, Uzbek, Kazak and Kirghiz tribesmen, as well as Mongolian and Chinese.

The name 'Turkestan' simply means land of the Turkomans, and for over two thousand years the Turkoman nomads have roamed this vast region, tending their herds, weaving their rugs and enjoying a lifestyle that has hardly changed in centuries. Yet despite its widely accepted cultural and territorial identity, Turkestan has never been an independent nation. As early as the 4th century AD the eastern part of Turkestan was annexed by the Chinese, and the subsequent centuries saw the region repeatedly conquered and divided, until at the beginning of the present century it was split between the USSR in the west and China in the east. This division is fundamental to the evolution of oriental rugs. Most carpet scholars accept that this region was the cradle, if not the actual birthplace, of rug-making; and just as there was an ongoing political division between the eastern and the western parts of the territory, so there was also a schism in the style and development of their rugs.

Turkoman weavings from West Turkestan (now Afghanistan and the former Soviet republics of Turkmenistan, Uzbekistan, Tadzhakistan, Kirghizstan and southern Kazakhstan) are noted for their dark red colouring and their use of repeating *gul* (p. 100) and stylized leaf or floral motifs. They are generally referred to as the 'red rugs' of Central Asia, and are often sold collectively as 'Bokharas'. As one moves westwards and southwards, the combined influence of Islam and Persian aesthetics becomes more apparent. Rugs increasingly reflect Islamic mythology and Persian designs, and, although each individual producing country or region modifies these schemes in keeping with its own cultural heritage, an underlying *Persian/Islamic* influence dominates the area of rug-making stretching from India in the east to the Balkans in the west.

In contrast, rugs from East Turkestan show a more general *Chinese* influence. Though the same designs predominate, the articulation of the forms and the minor infill decorations have a distinctly *Chinese* flavour. Similarly, the colour schemes reflect the *Chinese* preference for muted oranges, yellows and blues, rather than the richer reds and blues favoured by the weavers of West Turkestan. The *Chinese* influence becomes increasingly evident, the further east one goes; Buddhist and Taoist symbolism gradually supplants that of Islam, and many designs and colour schemes are drawn directly from Chinese culture and mythology.

When first approaching the subject of *Chinese* rugs, we should therefore think in terms of a 'Chinese sphere of influence', rather than a nation contained within fixed geographical boundaries. In reality, the cross-influences are enormously complex, and there are considerable differences between items from the various countries

Variations on the *ay-gul* medallion typical of East Turkestan rugs

and areas within the region as a whole. It is nevertheless a valid concept with which to begin an understanding of *Chinese* rugs.

Before embarking on a more detailed analysis of rug production throughout the Chinese sphere of influence, it is important to acquaint oneself with the different countries and regions involved. National borders have been in an almost constant state of flux for centuries, and some ancient and universally recognized countries (Tibet and Manchuria, for instance) no longer exist as independent nations. Others, like Mongolia, retain their separate national identity, but much of their traditional territory has been annexed by China.

It is also important to recognize that modern China is an amalgam of different countries and peoples; and that Chinese culture has evolved through its interaction with the cultures of other countries. Some things that we now think of as being intrinsically 'Chinese' were in fact probably introduced from such diverse sources as India, Egypt and, as some historians now believe, perhaps even as far away as Celtic Britain.

China, as we know it today, only came into existence after the formation of the People's Republic in 1949; and, since the annexation of Tibet and the return of Guandong (the southernmost part of Manchuria), in 1950, the current borders have remained more or less unchanged.

China is the third largest country in the world, slightly bigger than the USA, and occupies most of the habitable land in East Asia. Two-thirds of the total landmass is either mountainous or desert, and only about one-tenth is cultivated. The more fertile eastern region is irrigated by the three great river systems, the Yangtse (Chang-Jiang), the Yellow (Huang Ho) and the West (Hsi Chiang) rivers, and contains most of both the arable land and the densely populated urban conurbations. As one moves westwards, the country becomes more sparsely populated and forbidding. The northern border is guarded by the Gobi desert and the Altai mountains, and the southern border is dominated by the Himalayas and the Tibetan plateau. The most westerly territory of China is Sinkiang Uighur (Xinjiang Uygur) province, formerly known as 'East' or 'Chinese' Turkestan.

China's population is in excess of one thousand million (the largest of any country in the world) and includes, in addition to the Han Chinese, people of Mongol, Korean, Manchu, Tibetan, Turkic and other ethnic descent. The Han Chinese, who are themselves originally of mixed race, constitute approximately 94% of the total population

and are the people usually meant by the term 'Chinese'.

The ethnic complexity of modern China is reflected in the diversity of language and religion. Four major language families are represented (Sino-Tibetan, Altaic, Indo-European and Austroasiac), each with its own spectrum of individual languages (Han Chinese, Tibetan etc.), which are then further divided into numerous regional dialects (Mandarin, Cantonese, Fukien). The official tongue is Mandarin, and the majority of Chinese terms and place names in current use derive from this source.

Although China is officially atheist, Buddhism, Taoism and Confucianism still attract numerous adherents, and the influence of these traditional beliefs permeates every facet of Chinese culture (p. 52). In addition, there are long-established communities of Muslims, Roman Catholics and to a lesser extent Protestants.

East Turkestan, as the name suggests, is the eastern part of the ancient territory of Turkestan, situated between what was the Soviet Union to the west, and China to the east. It centres on the vast arid wastelands of the Tarim basin and is guarded to the north, west and south by high mountains. It is now fully incorporated into China, forming the 'Sinkiang Uighur (Xinjiang Uygur) Autonomous Region'. Despite its size, it has a population of less than 4 million and is the only territory of modern China that has not been heavily resettled by Han Chinese (see also p. 45).

Mongolia, one of the world's oldest countries, reached its zenith during the 12th and 13th centuries under the leadership of Genghis Khan and his successors (p. 47), when its influence extended from China in the east, to Hungary and Poland in the west. The Mongols were primarily herdsmen and warriors, whose culture and territorial ambitions were vital to the evolution of *Chinese* rugs. Today, their traditional homeland is divided into 'Outer' and 'Inner' Mongolia.

The former is an independent country, the sixth largest in Asia, bordered by Siberia to the north and China to the south, east and west. The terrain is ideal for nomadic herdsmen, with around five-sixths of the total landmass comprising vast grasslands and open plains, sandwiched between such natural barriers as the Gobi desert to the south and the Altai mountains to the west. This goes some way to explaining why it is only very recently that the traditional Mongolian lifestyle has begun to change. The official name of the country is now 'The Mongolian People's Republic', but it is usually referred to as Outer Mongolia, or simply Mongolia.

It has a population of under 2 million (making it one of the least densely populated countries in Asia), and its ethnic make-up is approximately 75% 'Khalkha' Mongols, 8% other Mongols and 5% Kazakh; the balance consists of small pockets of Russians, Chinese and people from other ethnic groups. The official language is Khalkha Mongolian (one of the nine major dialects of the Mongol language), although other dialects are also spoken, in addition to Russian and Chinese. The Mongolian 'Communist' government, since coming to power in 1921, has discouraged religious practice, but the influence of Tibetan Buddhism still pervades much of Mongolian culture and life.

Inner Mongolia is an area of vast steppe-lands, running the length of the southern border of Outer Mongolia. It was fully absorbed into China in 1947 and now constitutes the 'Nei Monggol Autonomous Region'. There are over 20 million people currently living in Inner Mongolia, with recent Chinese settlers now outnumbering the indigenous Mongols in a ratio of approximately ten to one.

Manchuria is the ancient home of the Manchus, a distinct ethnic group who have lived in this and adjacent regions for centuries, and who ruled China and its empire from the 17th century until the Chinese Revolution of 1912. The area that corresponds to ancient Manchuria is situated in the northeast corner of modern China. It was conquered by the Japanese in 1931 and returned to China in 1947. Since then it has been divided into the Chinese provinces of Liaoning, Jilin and Heilongjiang, and no longer appears on any maps as Manchuria.

The Manchus are a people of Tungus (Mongol) extraction who, at some point in their early history, interbred with a wide variety of other ethnic groups, including some of the Caucasian races who inhabited parts of Siberia in prehistoric times. They were referred to in Chinese records by a variety of names (the Juchen, Sushen and Eastern Barbarians), until the 16th century, when they became known as the 'Manchus'.

The direct antecedents of the Manchus (the Juchen) are known to have established an empire in Manchuria at the beginning of the 12th century. This was destroyed by the Mongols in 1234, and the surviving Juchen were driven into the northeast corner of Manchuria. They emerged three hundred years later as the 'Manchus', regained control over the whole of Manchuria, and by the mid-17th century had entered Peking and begun their conquest of China and the Chinese empire. The Manchu (Ch'ing) dynasty was established in 1644 and lasted until 1911, when the last emperor of the 'Celestial Empire', Hsuang T'ung (perhaps better known as P'u Yi, the five-year-old child who became the subject of the 1988 film *The Last Emperor*), was overthrown and a republic declared.

Tibet can be divided into two distinct, though inextricably connected, regions, which can perhaps best be described as 'Tibet proper' and 'cultural Tibet'. The former – an area almost the size of Spain, Italy and France combined – is a land of high plateaux and huge mountains, bounded by the Kunluns to the north and the Himalayas to the south. Not surprisingly for a country whose average altitude is 15,000 feet (4570 metres) above sea level, and which contains what is believed to be the highest inhabited town on earth, it is often referred to as 'the Roof of the World'. This clearly defined geographical area was ruled over by successive Dalai Lamas from their capital in Lhasa, before it was annexed by China in 1950, becoming the 'Chinese Autonomous Region of Xizang'.

'Cultural Tibet' (or 'ethnic Tibet', as it is sometimes called) is a vast region of Tibetan settlement that stretches north and east into what are now the Chinese provinces of

Sinkiang and Kansu, and southwards into Nepal, Bhutan, the Sikkim and Ladakh provinces of India and even parts of northern Burma. In the past, many of these areas were part of the Tibetan empire, but since the 16th and 17th centuries the territorial identity of Tibet has largely stayed within the borders associated with 'Tibet proper'.

The Tibetan people seem to have evolved from two different, though closely connected, ethnic groups, usually defined as the 'round-headed' and 'long-headed' groups. The former resemble the Mongols, Burmese and, to a lesser extent, the Chinese, and are found mainly in the cultivated river valleys of western and central Tibet. The latter are generally taller, more angular in build and possess more aquiline features. They predominate among the noble families in central Tibet and the nomads of the east and northeast.

All Tibetans speak the same language (Tibetan), and before the Chinese invasion 99.9% of the population was Buddhist. It is estimated that there are around $3\frac{1}{2}$ million Tibetans in 'Tibet proper' and another 4 million in 'cultural Tibet'; in addition, there are now somewhere in the region of 2 million refugees living in exile in India, Nepal and other parts of the world. Since the annexation, China has resettled much of Tibet; in 1991 the eastern provinces of Amdo and Kam saw Chinese settlers make up 72% and 62% of the total population, respectively. If this pattern continues, Tibetans are destined to become a minority people in their own land.

Nepal is an independent kingdom neighbouring Tibet in the north and India in the south. It was originally a group of small principalities, dominated by the Gurkhas from the 18th century until 1951, when King Tribhubana Bir Bikram established a cabinet system of government.

The population is approximately 17 million and is mainly comprised of people who originally descended from tribes of Indian, Tibetan and Central Asian ethnic groups. The official language is Nepali, although there are twelve other languages in common use, and the dominant religions are Hinduism (90%) and Buddhism (9%).

Although officially an independent constitutional monarchy, Nepal has close economic and political ties with India.

Ladakh, which roughly translated means 'land under the passes', is often referred to as 'Little Tibet' because of its close physical and cultural connections with that country. Ladakh is the most northwesterly state of India, bordered by Nepal, Tibet, China and Pakistan, and, due to its unusual climatic conditions, covers one of the strangest and most fascinating landscapes in the world. Imagine the Sahara desert 16,000 feet (4877 metres) above sea level, freezing cold and surrounded by ice-blue skies and snow-covered mountains, and you can begin to appreciate the unique qualities of Ladakh. It has a population of approximately 90,000, much of which is formed by people of Tibetan descent, and has absorbed thousands of more recent Tibetan refugees.

Sikkim is situated at the northeast tip of India, bordered by Tibet, Nepal and Bhutan. It is generally known as the 'Buddhist kingdom of India' and was an independent kingdom with British protectorate status until 1950, when this status was transferred to the newly independent India. In 1975 the monarchy was abolished, and Sikkim was fully absorbed into India. It currently has a population of approximately 315,000 people, including a significant number of Tibetan refugees.

Bhutan is a small independent monarchy situated in the eastern Himalayas between China to the north and India to the south, and is almost entirely surrounded by high mountains. From the 16th to the late 19th century Bhutan was largely under Tibetan rule. In 1865 the British government exercised a 'guidance' role over Bhutanese affairs. This continued until 1949, when a treaty was signed with India and, in effect, the Indian government assumed the role.

In addition to the indigenous Lepcha (a small ethnic group about which very little is known), the bulk of the population (60% and 25%, respectively) comprises people of Bhote (Tibetan) and Nepalese origins. The major religions are Buddhism (75%), Hinduism (20%) and Islam (5%).

The Silk Route

The 'Silk Route' is the name given to the overland trade route from China to Europe, which crossed the ancient territories of East Turkestan, Turkestan (West) and the Persian empire on its westward journey to Anatolia (Turkey), North Africa and the European countries beyond; it flowed like a huge meandering river through Central Asia, with tributaries branching off into India, Arabia and all the adjacent countries to the north and south (see pp. 8–9).

By the time the Venetian explorer Marco Polo traversed it in the late 13th century, it was a well-established trading link, bringing silks, spices and exotic foods and objects from China, India and other countries in the East, and taking Western artefacts and produce back along the same route. No one can say with any degree of certainty when exactly the 'Silk Route' first came into existence. We know from a combination of archaeological evidence and historical records that trade links between the Far East and the ancient kingdoms of Egypt, Mesopotamia and Babylonia had been established by the time of the Han Dynasty (206 BC–AD 220), and in all probability stretched back to the beginning of the 1st millennium BC, and perhaps beyond.

What is not so clear, however, is whether these early trade links were by land or sea. There is considerable evidence of ancient seafarers sailing down the Red Sea and Persian Gulf, and then crossing the Indian Ocean to India and the Far East. One interesting, but by no means conclusive argument in support of sea trade, is the similarity of the Chinese 'junk' (which the Chinese have used, relatively unchanged, for at least two thousand years) to the early Egyptian sailing vessels in operation during the 3rd millennium BC.

But even if, as seems likely, sea-routes were well established by the 1st and 2nd millennia BC, there is still the question of how trade took place with the vast territories inland. Merchants landing in northern Indian ports would still have faced a long and arduous journey across the Himalayas and the Takla Makan desert

before they were even close to the important trade centres of East Turkestan; and logic would seem to dictate a more direct overland route, rather than a combination of sea and land.

Whatever the precise nature of these early trading routes, excavations in the Takla Makan desert and the Tarim basin by archaeologist Sir Aurel Stein have uncovered ample physical evidence of cultural links between East Turkestan and Mesopotamia (and, by extension, Europe) during the 1st millennium BC. There is no doubt that East Turkestan, despite being one of the most barren and forbidding places on earth, had two things that its trading partners desired: gold and jade. The Altai mountains, literally meaning 'the mountains of gold', were so named because gold, silver, copper and other precious and semiprecious metals could be found in abundance. Jade was also endemic to the area, as were lapis lazuli, turquoise and other precious and semiprecious stones. The towns of Khotan, Kashgar and to a lesser extent Samarkand (all of which were later to play a crucial part in the evolution of rug-making in the Far East) became the centres of the jade and gold trade.

It is reasonable to conclude that ideas, beliefs and skills accompanied the raw materials and artefacts, helping, over the centuries, to forge the consciousness of all the peoples connected by the Silk Route. It would therefore be surprising if Chinese silk weavers had not learned from Persian textile weavers, and vice-versa; and if religious, mythological and thematic concepts, which would later resurface as design motifs, had not been interchanged.

The great migrations and conquests that spread across Asia in all directions (the Mongols of Genghis Khan, the Macedonian armies of Alexander the Great, the Huns, the Seljuk Turks and the great empires of the Persians, Moghuls and Ottomans) all brought an inevitable interchange of knowledge and beliefs. However, although conquests and migrations are vital factors in cultural interchange, they are by their very nature relatively short-lived. Once migrants have settled, or the conquering army has been expelled, their influence begins to wane; ideas and skills may be absorbed and developed by the host society, but ongoing stimulation is lost.

Trading links, in contrast, provide a constantly renewable source of contact, ensuring a perpetual updating of all the latest developments taking place in the societies en route. Consequently, the importance of the Silk Route in the history of oriental rugs cannot be emphasized too strongly. Although there is a great deal we do not understand about its early evolution, we do know that it provided a vital link between East and West for well over a thousand years, and that East Turkestan not only became the trading gateway, but also acted as both a buffer and a pivotal region between the two great spheres of influence: the *Persian* and the *Chinese*.

The Chinese language

Written Chinese, which can be traced back to the Shang Dynasty (*c.* 1766–1122 BC), is based on pictographs (simple pictorial images) which illustrate fundamental objects or actions (man, woman, bed, walking, sleeping etc.), and which can be combined with others to convey more complex concepts and abstract ideas (ideographs). For example, the combination of a woman and a child expresses the concept of 'goodness'. Similarly, juxtaposing the pictographs for 'mountain' and 'man' creates a compound ideograph that conveys not only the obvious allusion to a 'mountain-man', but also the concept of 'immortality', because, according to Taoist traditions, sages and immortals dwell in the mountains. Some of the concepts associated with compound ideographs are relatively easy to understand – the connection between a mother and child and 'goodness' is common to most cultures – but many others have their roots in the complex and often obscure mythologies of Chinese culture. Written Chinese has gradually evolved from its obvious pictorial roots into the more abstract 'characters' in use today, which rarely bear any resemblance to the objects they were originally intended to represent.

Individual characters (and ideographs) also have a phonetic significance, with each character representing a syllable or word, in the same way that the letters in European alphabets relate to both the written and spoken form of the language. Chinese, however, is far more complex. The syllable *yi*, for example, can be represented by over 215 characters. It is also common for the

Early Chinese ideographs: 'goodness' and 'communality'

same character to represent two or more words which sound identical, but have different meanings, in the same way that the word 'might', in English, can mean either 'possibly' or 'strength'.

Chinese also frequently uses different characters to illustrate subtle gradations in meaning of the same word: for example, the word *yuan* can be used to represent 'primary', 'origin' or 'source', and a different character is employed to show which specific meaning is intended. This complex interplay between the sound of a word and the meaning of all the characters that correspond to the same sound gives the Chinese language a tremendous capacity for puns and plays on words, which manifests itself in numerous areas of symbolism and superstition (p. 105).

Another result of this complex interplay between sounds and meanings is the number of characters needed to ensure that the language can keep pace with the constant evolution of concepts, inventions and events. It is estimated that there are now at least 50,000 characters in existence (if one includes both simple and compound ideographs); one kind of Chinese typewriter has a keyboard with 5400 characters.

There are several dialects of Han Chinese, the most influential of which, and the official language, is Mandarin. There has been a concerted attempt by the Chinese government to standardize the spoken language around Mandarin (the written language is similar across the dialects), and serious consideration has been given to adopting an alphabetic system of writing, which would bring Chinese into line with most other languages in the world. However, this system has run across entrenched opposition from those who fear that it represents an unacceptable break with the past.

Modern Chinese characters

Spelling and pronunciation

All translations from Chinese to other languages are, by necessity, strictly phonetic, and a number of 'romanizations' (transliterations into Latin-based and, generally, other European languages) have been attempted over the last two to three hundred years. The most widely used is the Wade-Giles system, a fusion of the work of Sir Thomas Wade and H.A. Giles, which gave us such familiar names as Peking and Shantung.

In the Wade-Giles system Chinese words and place names are pronounced more or less as they would be in English (i.e. Peking, Chung-king). In English-speaking and many other parts of the world, it is from this system that most traditional place and rug names are derived.

The pinyin system, introduced in 1979 as part of the Chinese government's attempt to unify the language, has begun to supersede the Wade-Giles system as the one in popular use. *Pinyin* replaced the traditional writing systems of Uighur, Jingpo, Kazakh and Lahu, and phoneticized all the Chinese languages, including previously unwritten ones; it also introduced diacritical (distinguishing) marks to show variations of sound not found in standard Han Chinese. As part of Chinese foreign policy, *pinyin* was recommended for use in all English-speaking countries, and 'Lessing', an alternative system, for use in German-speaking countries.

Pinyin pronunciation differs from the Wade-Giles system in several respects. In addition to subtle alterations in certain vowel sounds ('u' to 'o', as in Shantung/ Shandong, and 'e' to 'aa', as in Shensi/ Shaanxi, for example) several 'single' and 'compound' consonants are also changed. The letters 'p', 't' and 'j', in Wade-Giles, are normally replaced by 'b', 'd' and 'r', respectively, in *pinyin*, for example; 'hs' becomes 'x', and 'ch' changes to 'j' or 'zh'. Some letters in both systems are pronounced as they would be in English. Exceptions are included in the following list; the Wade-Giles version is shown in brackets:

b (p) as in *be*
c (ts, tz) similar to *its* or *zulu*
d (t) as in *dawn*
g (k) as in *go*
i (ih) as in *stir*
j (ch) as in *jeep*
o (o) as in *paw*
q (ch) as in *chap*
r (j) as in *read* or *azure*
u (u) as in *too*
x (hs) as in *ship*
z (ts, tz) as in *zero*
zh (ch) as in *jury*

ai (–) as in *pie*
ao (–) as in *cow*
ei (–) as in *hay*
ie (–) as in experi*e*nce
ou (–) as in *toe*

These pronunciations are only approximate; spoken Chinese depends on subtle variations of tone and emphasis being given to almost identical phonetic sounds, and a number of these have no direct equivalent in English or other European languages.

Place and rug names Most rug literature uses the Wade-Giles system of transliteration, and most rugs are marketed under their Wade-Giles name (Peking, Sinkiang, Tientsin). The Wade-Giles romanization of place and rug names has therefore been used throughout this book, with, where appropriate, the *pinyin* version accompanying it in brackets.

Direct comparison between the two systems is not always possible; some traditional towns, provinces and regions no longer exist as separate, identifiable locations, and entirely new towns and provinces have been formed. Those equivalents that can be given are shown on the map on pp. 128–9 and in the index; the *pinyin* version is provided in brackets.

Note that, because of the phonetic nature of all Chinese transliterations, slight variations in spelling may occur even within the same system; for example, Paotao and Paotow, Ning-Hsia and Ning-sia, in Wade-Giles.

How Chinese rugs get their names

Oriental rugs are traditionally named after the place where they were made or, in the case of nomadic items, the weaving tribe. For example, a rug made in the Persian (Iranian) town of Nain would be known as a 'Nain', and a rug produced by the nomadic Belouch tribe would be called a 'Belouch'. This system, however, only partially applies to Chinese rugs.

Items made before the mid-20th century are frequently named after specific towns or regions (Khotan, Paotao, Kansu), although they were not necessarily made in these places. Khotan, for example, was an important marketing town on the Silk Route, and rugs made by nomadic and semi-nomadic peoples throughout East Turkestan (Sinkiang) were traditionally sold in its bazaars. Over a period of time Khotan, and other major marketing towns,

became associated with certain styles and qualities of rug, but it is far from clear whether this was because these styles were exclusive to that particular town, or because of far more arbitrary factors. The same is true of China proper; Pekings and Suiyuans, for example, derive their names from the style and quality associated with the particular town, rather than because they were actually made there. Consequently, the exact attribution of old and antique *Chinese* rugs is often impossible, and, unless a definite provenance has been recorded, the names under which they are marketed should not be taken as proof of their origins.

The naming of modern rugs is even more confusing; only those made in Sinkiang (Xinjiang) province, formerly East Turkestan, bear any resemblance to the traditional rugs from the area in which modern versions are now produced; and even these may be marketed under a variety of names (p. 132). Rugs made in the rest of China are not normally connected to any style or quality traditionally associated with the producing region. Certain workshops may specialize in specific types or styles, but this is because they have developed an expertise in weaving these items, rather than because of any traditional local affinity with these kinds of rugs. It is perfectly normal for rugs marketed as 'Paotaos' or 'Pekings', for example, to be made hundreds of miles away from these towns. Some dealers may try to find out where a specific rug was made, but normally they will refer to it as an example of a particular 'range' (p. 131), or name it after its design (Aubusson) or a similar traditional weaving group (Peking). Alternatively, they may simply allocate any plausible Chinese name to give the rug a greater sense of 'individuality' than it would have if it were just called Chinese.

Although rugs are still marketed predominantly under their Wade-Giles names, they are also sometimes sold under their *pinyin* version, and confusion may arise as to whether an attribution refers to a different style of rug or is simply an alternative spelling of the same name.

Chinese weaving groups

The term 'weaving group' can be applied to any weaving centre or tribe that produces its own distinctive rugs. It is not enough for rugs to be produced in the same town, or by the same ethnic group; they must also share the same basic visual and structural characteristics. In Iran, for example, rugs made in the town of Isfahan are said to belong to the 'Isfahan' group because they are all very similar in character. In contrast, rugs made in Lahore (Pakistan) are rarely considered part of a 'Lahore' weaving group because of the diversity of weaving styles employed in the town.

The term may be used for both 'general' and 'specific' attributions: for example, rugs from the Hamadan region in Iran are known collectively as Hamadans, but may also be attributed to individual village weaving groups (Tuisarkan, Mazlaghan etc.).

Chinese weaving groups are judged by the same criteria. However, because *Chinese* weaving did not grow from clearly established village and regional roots, from which individual rug styles and characteristics could evolve and be consolidated (as it did in many other rug-making countries), the criteria for establishing individual weaving groups are fairly loose, and the attribution of older rugs is often arbitrary (p. 117). Be especially wary of specific attributions. Rugs marketed in East Turkestan, for example, can normally be accepted as originating from that region (although they are sometimes confused with Mongolian rugs); but, unless a clear provenance is recorded, one should be sceptical about attributions to specific towns (e.g. Khotan, Yarkand). The term 'weaving group' should only be used in reference to old and antique rugs. There are no contemporary Chinese weaving groups; all rugs are now defined by ranges (p. 131).

Rugs and carpets

The terms 'rug' and 'carpet' are normally used to denote size, a carpet being any rug with a surface area larger than about $47\,\text{ft}^2$ $(4.4\,\text{m}^2)$, and whose length is less than $1\frac{1}{2}$ times its width. This distinction is generally only made in Britain and Commonwealth countries. In the United States, and most other countries, the word 'rug' is used to describe any item, regardless of size. In general, however, the terms are interchangeable, and will be used as such throughout this book. An exception will be made when size is being discussed; the terms will then be used in accordance with the British convention.

Runners, strips and mats

The first two terms refer to items that are long and narrow – usually where the length is over $2\frac{1}{2}$ times the width – and are often used in place of the word 'rug': i.e. a Chinese runner or Sinkiang strip. There are no firm rules defining the difference between the two, although in general a runner is of corridor or hallway size, while a strip is rather smaller, rarely more than $3' \times 1'$ $(0.9 \times 0.3\,\text{m})$. The term 'mat' can be used to describe any small rug, but normally refers only to items less than $2' \times 2'$ $(0.6 \times 0.6\,\text{m})$.

Collections of Chinese rugs

There are very few substantial public collections of old and antique *Chinese* rugs outside China. However, the Metropolitan Museum of Art, New York, and the Textile Museum, Washington, D.C., have outstanding examples. Other excellent collections can be found in the Royal Ontario Museum, Canada; the Österreichisches Museum für Angewandte Kunst, Vienna; the Museum für Kunsthandwerk, Frankfurt; and the Muraltengut and the Museum Reitberg, Zurich.

The Victoria and Albert Museum in London houses the famous 'studio collection' of late Ch'ing Dynasty rugs, though, sadly, this collection can normally be seen only by appointment. There are several museums throughout Europe and North America with a few fine examples on show; and the Japanese Imperial Treasure House, Shosoin, at Nara, has a remarkable collection of *Chinese* weavings, including pileless rugs, dating from the 1st millennium AD.

Chapter II

How Chinese rugs are made

All *Chinese* rugs are made in one of three ways: knotting, tufting or weaving. The first two techniques produce pile rugs, which form the bulk of Chinese production and are the main focus of this book. The Chinese also produce flatweaves, needlepoint and petit point embroideries, which, although not generally classified as rugs will also be discussed (p. 29).

Warps and wefts
Warps and wefts are the basic constituents of all textiles, and in rugs are generally referred to as the 'foundation'. The strands of yarn running lengthways from top to bottom of a rug, culminating in the fringes at either end, are known as the 'warp'; those running widthways across the rug, forming the 'selvedges' on either side, are the 'weft'. Usually, both the warp and weft are made of the same material, but it is not unknown for different materials to be used – a cotton warp with a silk weft, for example.

Selvedges and fringes
The selvedges – the sides, or edges, of the rug – are formed by wrapping the weft strands around the last few warp strands, usually reinforced by stitching, in order to secure the rug tightly across its width.

Fringes are continuations of the warp strands, which are secured in a variety of ways to hold the rug firmly at the top and bottom. Tied fringes, the most common in all styles of *Chinese* rug, are formed by tying two or more warp strands into a knot that presses tightly against the final weft strand, and then repeating the process across the whole width of the rug. In kelim (or plaited) fringes, another popular method, interweaving of the warp and weft strands continues beyond the point where the pile stops, producing a short length of kelim at either end of the rug.

Looms
Although looms differ considerably in size and complexity, they all operate on the same basic principle, which requires a secure frame on which to tie the warp strands. Looms may be made of wood or metal, or a combination of both, and either of fixed dimensions, or have one or more sides adjustable. The type of loom places limitations on the size and, to a lesser degree, sophistication of the rugs that can be produced.

All contemporary *Chinese* rugs are made on vertical looms; some are relatively simple, fixed rectangular frames, but the majority are more sophisticated, adjustable looms. Old and antique *Chinese* rugs may have been made on either vertical looms or horizontal looms. East Turkestan, Mongolia and Manchuria had predominantly nomadic cultures until the 19th century, and it is only in the last hundred years that a fully settled way of life has taken hold. It is therefore highly probable that a number of rugs from these areas were woven on horizontal (nomadic) looms.

In China proper, however, where a more settled, agrarian lifestyle had been in force for centuries, it is almost certain that the vast majority of rugs were woven on vertical (village) looms.

Whether a rug has been woven on a vertical or horizontal loom is of no importance in determining its commercial value. Nor are there any intrinsic differences in the aesthetic or technical merits of items produced on either type of loom.

Horizontal (nomadic) looms are the most simple and primitive in contemporary use, and have changed little since their invention several millennia ago. They normally consist of four wooden beams laid out flat to form a rectangle, and then secured by pegs driven into the ground. This method of weaving is compatible with the nomadic lifestyle, allowing unfinished rugs to be left attached to an opposite pair of beams, rolled into bundles and strapped to the back of a horse or camel for transportation to the next encampment, where they can then be easily reassembled. The limitations of this type of loom lie in the physical constraints it places on the weaver, who is unable to reach more than a couple of feet across the rug from any side. This makes it difficult to produce large rugs or those with intricate designs. Consequently, nomadic rugs usually employ relatively simple, angular designs, and there may be occasional lapses in symmetry and articulation, often adding to their 'ethnic' charm.

Vertical (village) looms are only marginally more sophisticated than horizontal looms, and are constructed from two vertical beams (usually secured on a base or fixed into the ground), with two horizontal beams attached to the verticals. This arrangement allows the weaver access across the entire width of the rug, allowing wider items to be produced and making it slightly easier to weave more intricate designs.

Adjustable looms are vertical looms in which one or more of the beams (usually on the vertical axis) can be moved in order to increase the inner dimensions of the loom. This enables larger items to be produced and makes it easier to weave intricate designs. There are several variations on this type of loom in general use in China today. Tabriz looms have a 'shuttle' beam which, by altering the tension on the warp strands, shifts the finished work to the rear of the loom, so that the weaver is able to sit in the same position during the entire weaving process. Roller looms operate on the same principle, but the warp strands are attached to a rotary mechanism that winds the finished work onto a roller, allowing even larger items to be produced.

Tools

These may vary in size and construction, and individual weavers may have several slightly different versions of each, but they are all basically the same.

A knife is used to cut the threads of the pile

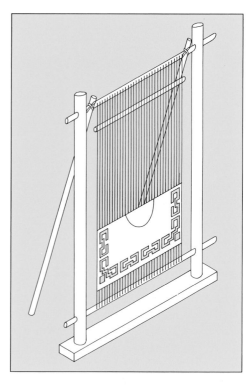

A simple vertical loom

and the warp and weft; the blade usually terminates in a hook, which is used to help form the knot for the pile.

A beating comb, consisting of a series of splayed metal teeth set into a wooden or metal base (not dissimilar to a large hair-comb), is used to beat (or tighten) the weft threads against the finished row of knots, ensuring the compactness of the rug.

Shears are used to clip the pile to an even level once the rug has been completed. Over the last few decades, manual shears have largely been replaced by electrical shears. These are now standard equipment in contemporary Chinese weaving, but some rugs woven outside China (e.g. Nepal, Sikkim, Ladakh) may be clipped using manual shears.

Incising tools are also used in order to produce a 'chiselled' or 'sculpted' effect (p. 27). These are usually small rotary cutters, or narrow-headed versions of electrical shears.

Materials

Chinese rugs normally use only natural fibres, and any rug containing synthetic materials will almost certainly have been machine-made. A small minority of old and antique items use metallic (gold, silver) thread interwoven with wool or silk.

Wool is the best and most widely used rug-making material. It is soft, durable, easy to work, and contains natural oils, such as lanolin, which resist dirt, making wool relatively simply to clean. Good carpet wool needs to combine softness with durability and a degree of springiness, otherwise the rug will wear out quickly or fail to return to its natural shape if creased or depressed. As a general rule, the best wool comes from lambs between eight and fourteen months old, particularly those from colder, harsher highland regions.

China proper is not a noted wool-producing country (although a number of its provinces have wool-producing areas), but it has traditionally had access to Tibetan, Mongolian, Kansu and Sinkiang (East Turkestan) wool. The wool from these regions, mainly derived from the 'fat-tailed' sheep, is considered amongst the finest rug-making wool in the world. It is normally divided into three grades: Sining wool from Tibet, a long-stapled wool known in the trade as 'spinning' wool; Mongolian and Kansu wool, a short-stapled wool, referred to as 'filling' wool; and Sinkiang wool, another short-stapled filling wool, which was traditionally 'river-washed' before being transported to the other weaving regions. For much of this century the Chinese have also imported wool from such countries as Britain, New Zealand and Australia.

In addition to sheep's wool, a number of older *Chinese* rugs also used goat, yak and Bactrian camel wool and hair. These are rarely found in contemporary *Chinese* rugs, with the exception of the Chinese goat-wool range (p. 135) and items produced by semi-nomads in the border regions and by ethnic Tibetans in India and Nepal. Most contemporary Chinese rugs are made with wool from various different countries and native regions, with each range (Standard Chinese, Sinkiang, etc.) employing a specific wool combination. The quality of the wool also varies slightly between grades within the same range. However, the overall standard of wool in all *Chinese* carpets is good, and in general the higher the grade of rug, the better the quality of wool employed.

Yarn is produced by spinning wool fibres, either by hand or machine, into a continuous thread, which is twisted, in opposing directions, with other threads to form a continuous strand. (Machine-spinning is the norm in contemporary Chinese weaving, but some Tibetan rugs still use hand-spun yarns.) The individual threads are referred to as the 'ply' (a yarn made up of three threads is called 3-ply), and, as a rule, the more 'ply' that go into a yarn, the thicker and stronger it will be.

Cotton grows in China and has been in plentiful supply for centuries, providing a natural resource for the textile industry. It is normally only used as a foundation material (i.e. for warps and wefts) in *Chinese* carpets. There are a handful of old items with a cotton pile (one of the most famous is in the Vienna Museum), but the vast majority of contemporary Chinese rugs have wool or silk piles. Cotton has numerous advantages as a foundation material; it is stronger, more vermin-resistant, and keeps its shape better than wool; and because it is thinner, it can also be used for finer weaving. It is, however, susceptible to mildew.

Silk is produced by a species of moth (*bombyx mori*) commonly known as the silkworm. It is native to China and has been employed in Chinese textiles and rug-making for centuries. Two kinds of silk are used in weaving: raw silk, also known as 'drawn' or 'reeled' silk, because it is drawn directly from the cocoon; and waste silk, derived from damaged cocoons, which has to be carded and spun like wool or cotton. Most *Chinese* silk rugs use waste silk.

As a pile material, silk has the advantage of combining durability with wonderful aesthetic and textural qualities. It is extremely strong and can be spun into the very thin strands needed for exceptionally fine knotting. In many ways it embodies the opposite properties to wool, being cool (both tactually and visually) as opposed to warm, *yin* as opposed to *yang*, reflecting rather than absorbing light. These properties also have a mystical significance, imbuing it with the power to repel (reflect back) malevolent psychic forces; silk garments traditionally protect the wearer from spells, and strategically placed silk or reflective objects are used to ward off evil influences. Silk is more expensive than wool and has the disadvantage of scuffing more easily and melting if it comes into contact with flames or excessive heat. Silk rugs therefore require more care to protect them from damage, and should always be rolled rather than folded, as they tend to retain creases in the pile.

Mercerized cotton, which is occasionally used as a pile material, is normally referred to as 'artificial', or 'art', silk.

Dyeing and colours

Dyeing is as important to the appeal and quality of a finished carpet as the weaving and the design. If the colour scheme is imbalanced, or the dyes are fugitive, the entire rug can be spoiled. Rug-producers realize that as many people buy rugs for their colour schemes as for their designs, and so take great care in both the choice of dyes and the execution of the dyeing process.

This usually begins after the yarn has been cleaned, normally by washing in a weak solution of soda and soap. It is then immersed in an alum, uric acid or other 'mordant' solution (a chemical used to help bond the dye to the fibre) for up to twelve hours, before being soaked in a bath of dye.

Natural, or vegetable dyes derive from a number of vegetable, animal and mineral sources, some of which are intrinsically fugitive, although many produce a quality of tone, particularly as they mellow with age, that is unsurpassed by any chemical alternatives. Commercially, however,

some natural dyes have the disadvantage of being expensive and difficult to obtain; and even something as cheap and plentiful as indigo does not always produce exactly the same shade, because of the differing amounts of pigment in each plant. Many collectors cherish this inconsistency as an integral part of a rug's individuality and charm, but large importers and department stores demand a standard of quality control that leaves little scope for such variations. Natural dyes were used exclusively in all *Chinese* rugs until the end of the 19th century; since then there has been a steady increase in the use of chemical dyes, although a few items, especially authentic Tibetan, still rely on natural dyes.

Blue is derived from the ubiquitous indigo plant (*polygonum tinctorum*), which, apart from producing a wide variety of beautiful and stable shades, also helps to preserve the pile material, possibly because it is the only pigment that is colourfast without the addition of a mordant, which can undermine wool or silk. Red usually comes from the madder plant (*rubia tinctorum*), but other shades may be obtained from the crushed bodies of the female 'cochineal' insect (*dactylopius coccus*), or another insect *chermes abietis*. Yellow comes from the pistils of the saffron crocus, which is now rare and very expensive, or from a variety of other plants such as *sophora japonica, gardenia jasminoides*, vine leaves, rhubarb, turmeric and varieties of the reseda plant. Black is made from pomegranate peel, or flour broth, often combined with iron rust. Tan and light brown are usually made from acorn cups. Purple and purplish red are derived from sumac (a mixture of dried and powdered leaves from certain plants traditionally used in dyeing and tanning).

Other colours are created from a wide range of plants, barks, nutshells, berries, insects, minerals and earth, and by combinations of primary colours.

Synthetic dyes are used almost exclusively in contemporary *Chinese* carpets. The first synthetic 'aniline' dye, fuchsine, was derived from benzene by an English chemist in 1856; three years later a French chemist produced a similar violet dye (mauveine). These discoveries were followed by the rapid development of other cheap, mass-produced pigments. Unfortunately, many were unattractive and fugitive, and were banned in several carpet-weaving countries. China, however, continued to use them, and they can be found in a number of items made during the late 19th and early 20th centuries.

The discovery of 'chrome' dyes, between the First and Second World Wars, changed attitudes towards synthetic dyes. They were far more stable and visually attractive, and they had the same advantages of low cost and availability as aniline dyes. From the mid-20th century onwards they were in general use throughout the Chinese sphere of influence, and today's buyer can be assured that colours, whether synthetic or natural, will be stable and generally improve with age.

Abrash is the term used to describe a sudden change in the intensity of a particular colour that does not correspond to a logical change in design. It is usually caused by changing to a new batch of separately dyed yarn part-way through the weaving of a rug. The colour often looks the same when new, but as it begins to age, the two batches may fade at different rates. Abrashes are common and perfectly acceptable in village and nomadic items, often adding a rough-hewn beauty and individuality, but they are not acceptable in workshop rugs. Any contemporary *Chinese* rug with sudden changes in colour should be considered flawed or damaged, the only exceptions being authentic ethnic rugs made outside China, and those Chinese rugs, such as a number of Sinkiangs, that are made deliberately to echo older, more tribal items.

Mellowness is the term used to describe colours that have lost their initial tonal intensity and faded to softer shades. Traditionally, when rugs were taken off the loom, the colours were bright and garish, and it took several years before exposure to sunlight created the optimum 'mellowness'. Today, rugs are frequently chemically washed to create this effect (p. 28).

The relationship between colour and age
Colours fade through exposure to sunlight, and it is often assumed that the more the colours have faded, the older the rug will be. While this assumption has some validity, remember that colours fade faster in strong light, so the degree of fading may reflect the strength of the light source rather than the age of the rug. Chemical washing has a similar effect, and a useful (though by no means foolproof) way of judging whether colours have mellowed naturally is to look into the pile of the rug: if the tone is the same from the surface to the root of the pile, the colours have almost certainly been bleached by chemical washing; if the colours are deeper at the root than on the surface, they have probably faded due to the action of light (pp. 28, 35).

The meaning of individual colours In China the meaning and mystical significance of individual colours are just as profound and complex as for motifs and designs. Certain colours are associated with specific qualities or spiritual forces. Red, for example, is observed in fire and the rising sun, and is therefore associated with life and vitality; blue, in contrast, being the colour of the sky and water, represents heaven, and governs such qualities as serenity, purity and harmony. This linkage between the quality of fire and the colour of fire, for example, is common to most cultures, but the Chinese take the association one step further; if the sun, being red, represents life and vitality, then it follows that anything red will share in the sun's life-giving qualities. Consequently, red plants, animals, minerals and mythological creatures will all contain to some degree the 'soul substance' (p. 104) of fire and the sun. This belief extends into Chinese medicine, where bodily organs are connected to specific colours, and any plant, mineral or animal of the same colour is credited with possessing a natural tonic for that organ. Healers would search 'dragon-haunted' pools after thunderstorms for fossilized bones of the appropriate colour. These 'dragon bones' were placed in a medicinal pecking order; five-coloured ones were best, followed by white and yellow, and then black.

Evolution of the dragon: from the simplified Shang Dynasty symbol to the more
elaborate, highly stylized versions of later dynasties

In Chinese symbolism the five primary colours correspond to the five colours of the dragon (p. 107). The Chinese believe that the immortal dragon displays all five colours, but dragons normally display only one predominant colour, which is associated with specific objects and qualities.

Yellow dragons are connected with earth, lightning, flames and the sun. Yellow warms the blood and promotes growth; it contains the sacred blend of sun-fire, lunar-fire and moisture, and symbolizes the mystery of life and immortality. It is the sacred colour of Buddhism (evolved souls are said to radiate yellow auras when they reach *nirvana*). According to tradition, several shades of yellow were worn at the imperial court, and skilled observers were reputed to be able to judge a man's status by the particular shade of his tunic; 'imperial yellow' was reserved for the emperor. In Chinese medicine, yellow is associated with the spleen (traditionally the seat of pensiveness) and the stomach, and also represents the last month of summer.

Red dragons are connected with fire, the sun and the planet Mars. Red represents summer; it possesses the *yang* properties of vitality and joy, and also a cruder, more corporeal essence of life. In Chinese medicine, red corresponds to the heart (the seat of joy) and the large intestine, and, in its manifestation as a bird, governs summer and the south.

Blue dragons are connected with the *yin* qualities of peace, serenity and harmony, associated with the east, water, the sky and the Great Mother; in its greener shades, blue is linked to the 'mysterious substance that gives plants life' and, by extension, underpins the symbolism of jade. Medically, it corresponds to the liver (the seat of anger) and gall bladder, and governs wood, spring and the planet Jupiter.

White dragons are connected with the moon, stars and day, and are often associated with the 'pure' aspect of the Great Mother, represented by pearls, shells, dew and white jade. In their manifestation as 'white tigers', they are also associated with the west, autumn, wind, metal and the planet Venus. White is the colour of mourning, and in medicine relates to the lungs (the seat of grief) and the small intestines.

Black dragons govern night, darkness and the Otherworld, and, in their manifestation as a tortoise, are associated with the north, winter, cold, rain and drought. Medically, they relate to the kidneys (the seat of fear) and the bladder.

Further information on colour symbolism can be found in Chapter V (p. 97).

Knotted, or pile rugs

In *Chinese* (as in most other oriental) rugs, the pile is created by tying a short length of yarn around two or more adjacent warp strands, so that the ends protrude upwards to form the surface (or pile) of the rug. This process is known as 'knotting', because when the warp and weft strands have been beaten together to hold the yarn firmly in place, a securely tied knot is formed. Every knot corresponds to two individual strands of pile, and a skilled weaver can tie up to a thousand individual knots per hour. Once the warp strands have been fastened to the loom, knots are tied across pairs of warp strands, working from the outer edge in a horizontal row across the whole width of the rug. Sometimes the knots are tied across more than two warp strands, but this practice weakens the rug. These inferior types of knot, known as *jufti* or *langri* – literally 'old woman' – are fortunately quite rare in *Chinese* carpets. Once one horizontal row of knots has been completed, they are secured by one or more weft strands (usually two) and then beaten tightly together with the weaver's comb. The process continues up the length of the rug.

Different types of knot are used throughout the rug-making world, but they all do essentially the same job, and none is fundamentally superior to any other. However, knowing which type of knot has been used can be very useful in determining a rug's attribution; weavers often copy designs from other groups, but they rarely, if ever, change the knot they use.

The Senneh, or Persian knot is formed by looping the pile yarn through two warp

To obtain the correct knotting sequence, the weavers follow motifs mapped out on graph paper

strands and then drawing it back through one. It is often referred to as the 'asymmetrical' knot because the pile yarn may be drawn to either the left or the right of the warp strands. Some authorities argue that it is easier to articulate detailed, curvilinear designs using the Senneh knot, but this is not universally accepted, and there are numerous examples of intricate designs being produced successfully using other types of knot. The Senneh knot is the one most frequently found in all contemporary Chinese carpets.

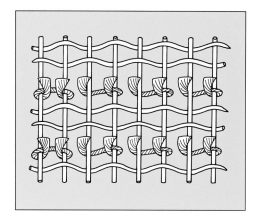

In Chinese rugs a Ghiordes knot is generally used to secure the lefthand edge, while the rest of each row is composed of Senneh knots

The Ghiordes, or Turkish knot is formed by looping the pile yarn through two warp strands and then drawing it back through the inside of both warps. It is often called the 'symmetrical' knot and is reputed to produce extremely compact rugs. Again, this is not universally accepted, and rugs made with other knots may be equally compact. In Chinese rugs, the Ghiordes knot is frequently used as a 'securing' knot on the extreme edges, the rest of the rug being woven using the Senneh knot. It is also the predominant knot in Tibetan weaving (p. 29).

The fineness of the knotting

This refers to the number of individual knots that have been tied to form the pile of a rug, and is taken by many rug dealers as the ultimate criterion of quality (i.e. the more knots there are, the better the rug must be). This is simply not true. The quality of a rug should be judged by a combination of structural and aesthetic factors, in addition to its knot-count (p. 34). Most *Chinese* rugs are not particularly finely knotted, but they are nevertheless generally very well made and durable, and employ relatively simple designs that do not require a high knot-count for their visual success. Where 'fineness' becomes important is in the articulation of very intric-

ate, curvilinear designs; and the more intricate the design, the more knots are needed. Consequently, in rugs that employ similar intricate designs, a 240-line version will normally be superior to one woven in a 160-line grade.

The fineness of Chinese rugs is usually measured in 'lines', which correspond to the number of knots running horizontally along a linear foot. In most weaving countries, fineness is measured in knots per in^2, or m^2, and calculated by counting the number of knots along a linear inch (or metre) on both the horizontal and vertical axes of a rug, and then multiplying them together. For example, if there are 10 knots running horizontally, and 10 running vertically along a linear inch, the rug would be graded as having 100 knots per in^2. The individual knots can, with a little practice, be quite easily discerned on the back of the rug, as they form small bumps where the pile yarn has been tied around the warp strands.

Converting 'lines' into 'knots per in^2' is necessary when comparing the relative knot-counts of *Chinese* and non-*Chinese* rugs, and requires only a fairly simple calculation. The first step is to divide the number of lines by 12 to find the number of knots along a linear inch – a 120-line carpet, for example, will have 10 knots per linear inch ($120 \div 12 = 10$). Then multiply the number of knots per linear inch by itself ($10 \times 10 = 100$), and call the result 'knots per in^2'.

Converting 'knots per in^2' to 'lines' is achieved by reversing the calculation. First, find the square root of the number of knots per in^2, and then multiply by 12. For example, 400 knots per in^2 ($\sqrt{400} = 20 \times 12 = 240$) is equivalent to 240-lines. Exact comparisons are difficult because the number of knots along the vertical and horizontal axes is not always the same, but it nevertheless provides a useful guideline.

Closed- and open-back rugs

Chinese hand-knotted rugs are divided into those woven in 'closed' and 'open' back techniques, which differ only in the way the knots are held in relation to the weft.

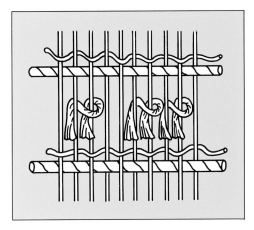

Open-back weaving

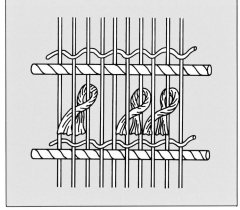

Closed-back weaving

Open-back rugs form the bulk of all *Chinese* production, and are represented in every range, quality and style. They employ the standard oriental rug-weaving technique, in which the knot is looped over the first (thicker) weft strand without changing its position in relation to the second (thinner) weft. An open-back rug is slightly more flexible than a closed-back one, and can often be identified by the traces of weft strands (usually white) running in horizontal lines across the back.

Closed-back rugs are found in the Standard Chinese and, to a lesser degree, some other contemporary Chinese ranges; they differ from the open-back technique in that the knots are drawn back under the first (thicker) weft. This gives the rugs a stiffer feel and conceals the weft strands, so that they cannot be seen from the back; it produces extremely compact, tightly woven items. In ranges where both techniques are employed, closed-back rugs are slightly more expensive and are generally accepted as being of better quality.

Clipping

Once a rug has been woven, its pile is clipped (or cut) to the required length. The first rough clipping is normally done by the weaver with a pair of scissors whilst the rug is still on the loom; this takes the pile down to approximately $1/8''$ (3 mm) longer than its final length. Specialist craftsmen then run electric shears backwards and forwards over the rug, clipping about $1/100''$ (0.3 mm) at each sweep, until the pile is both perfectly smooth and even, and the correct length.

The pile length in Chinese rugs varies from range to range, and there are often different lengths of pile available from rugs within the same range, including those employing the same designs (see Chapter VII). Pile length is not in itself an indication of quality, but the Chinese follow the standard rule for all oriental rugs, which is that simple, bold designs work with any length of pile, but intricate designs are usually only successful on short-pile rugs.

Incising and sculpturing In addition to clipping, some contemporary *Chinese* rugs also have their piles 'sculptured' or 'incised', so that certain motifs – usually the main ones in the design – appear to be raised above the rest of the rug, giving the pile an 'embossed' effect. The technique is normally only used on items (from the Standard Chinese range, for example) that employ simple, bold designs. It tends to follow three stages. The first, called *kai-huang* (literally 'opening the wilderness'), consists of making a thin incision around selected elements in the design. This is then deepened and widened, in a process called 'sloping' (*pian*), to create a contoured effect around each motif. After the rug has been washed, the final stage, known as 'incising' (*tougou*, 'rinsing the furrows'), refines and clarifies the sculpturing.

It is not clear how or when this technique was first introduced into *Chinese* weaving, but examples of sculpturing are found in a number of old and antique items, and it has long been widely used in Tibetan rugs.

Washing

Once the weaving, clipping and, where applicable, the sculpturing have been completed, the rug is washed to remove surface dirt and excess dye, to loosen and straighten the pile, and to give it its characteristic 'finish'. Old rugs were simply washed in soap and water, but most contemporary ones are now soaked (or 'washed') in a chemical solution.

Chemical washing normally includes some form of moth-proofing, but its main purpose is to give a specific 'finish', or patina, to the pile; it frequently reproduces the effects of age by toning down the colours and imitating the gloss or sheen that results from the accumulated friction between the pile and the soles of slippers and shoes. Certain types of wool (e.g. Tibetan) have a natural sheen, but most rugs would require years of use to achieve this effect; chemical washing provides an immediate shortcut.

Several variations are possible by altering the chemical formula, and each contemporary range has its own distinctive finish. However, careless or excessive use of chemicals can damage the pile, making it less resistant to wear and tear; it may also enable the producer to get away with using inferior wools and dyes, which would be instantly recognizable if the rug were unwashed.

Sometimes the rug is washed in the workshop where it was made, or at a specialized facility in the country of origin, but it is increasingly common for rugs to be exported unwashed and then be given their 'chemical treatment' by the large importers in the West, who can tailor the finish to the tastes of each specific market.

Tapestry weaving

This is something of a misnomer, because the items marketed by the Chinese as 'tapestries' are almost always extremely finely knotted pile rugs, employing intricate pictorial designs, and not tapestries in the Western sense of the term. The main difference is that tapestries frequently use multicoloured yarn for their knots.

Hooking and tufting

In hooked and tufted rugs the pile is produced by pushing yarn through a duckcloth or hessian backing material. The back of the rug is then sealed with latex to keep the yarns in place, and normally covered with a cloth backing. Any Chinese rug with a cloth backing will almost certainly have been made in this way. Although these items are technically handmade, they are not hand-knotted, and should never be passed off as authentic oriental rugs. It is extremely important always to check the back of a rug, because of the substantial difference, in both quality and price, between these items and authentic hand-knotted rugs. Hooked and tufted rugs are perfectly acceptable, as long as their inferior quality is reflected in the price.

Hooking was a method of rug-making popular in Europe and North America during the last century. The basic technique involves hooking or threading torn strips of fabric through a hessian or burlap backing with the aid of a large needle, and then drawing them back so as to create small loops on the surface. A variant technique, known as 'latch-hooking', in which the loop is cut, creates a more orthodox pile rug effect. Many older examples of these 'rag rugs' have now become collectable in their own right. The Chinese rug-making industry adopted and refined Western hooking techniques, often using multicoloured yarn to heighten the design, and now produces both 'loop' and 'cut' pile versions in a wide variety of colour schemes and designs.

Tufting works on a similar principle, but the pile yarn is fired through the cloth backing using a tufting gun. The majority of these items are made in very similar designs to those employed by hand-knotted rugs, and the unwary buyer could easily purchase one without realizing that it was not a genuine oriental rug.

Other weaving techniques

Flatweaves, or kelims

Flatwoven rugs are generally referred to as kelims (or *gelims*), which is a Turkish word for prayer rug. There are a number of different flatweaving techniques, but they are all based on the principle of interweaving the warp and weft strands to create a flat, pileless surface. Kelim weaving is done in sections, not in horizontal rows, as in pile rugs, and the design is created by using different-coloured weft strands for each colour segment, rather than inserting additional pieces of yarn. The most common weaving method, known generally as 'warp-sharing', broadly consists of interweaving each individual coloured weft strand through a specific number of warp strands (rather than from edge to edge) and then securing them around common warp threads in a staggered formation. This ensures that the rug is held together by the counter-tension of at least two sections of weft pulling against the same warp strand in opposite directions.

Alternative techniques include stitching together each separately woven portion of the design. In all kelims, the different-coloured weft strands that form the pattern on the face of the rug are also clearly visible from the back.

Needlepoint and petit point

These are produced by stitching (or embroidering) a design on a piece of cloth, usually cotton, using different-coloured threads: a technique developed in the West and adopted by the Chinese. The term

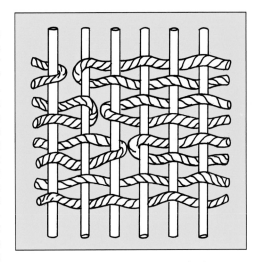

Kelim weaving, using a warp-sharing technique

'point' refers to the number of stitches running along a linear inch, so a 10-point item – the standard quality in Chinese needlepoint – employs 10 stitches per inch. As with other types of embroidery, the design is intended to be seen only from the front, and the back is usually covered by a piece of plain cloth.

In needlepoint, the background and the motifs are produced with the same number of stitches. In petit point, the background employs a standard number of stitches, while the motifs are created using a finer stitch – i.e. more stitches per inch. A typical example would be a 10-point background with individual motifs in a 24-point (or more) stitch.

Tibetan weaving

Separate mention must be made of Tibetan weaving, because it employs its own unique method of knotting, as well as its own range of dyestuffs and modified loom.

The Tibetan loom differs from the standard loom in that it normally employs fixed beams on both the vertical and horizontal (A) axes, and two (or more) adjustable beams, or rods, on the horizontal axis (B). This is necessary because the warp strands

are looped around the beams in a complex counter-locking pattern, enabling the tension of the warp strands to be altered by placing different-sized wedges behind the adjustable beams. (See p. 30).

Tibetan weaving employs a standard Ghiordes (Turkish) knot on the extreme lefthand pair of warps, but the Tibetan weaver will then switch to a piece of yarn long enough to make several knots, looping

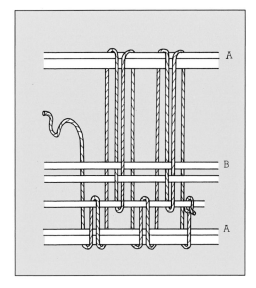

The Tibetan method of laying the warp:
A fixed beams, B adjustable rods

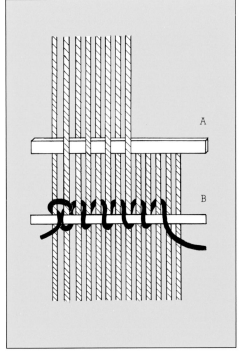

The Tibetan system of knotting:
A adjustable beam,
B weaving rod

it around pairs of warp strands and over a 'weaving rod' until it runs out, or until he reaches a part of the design where another colour is required. The loose end is then pulled tight and tied, and the gauge-rod removed, leaving a row of securely tied knots which are trimmed to open the pile. This process is repeated across the width of the rug, with a weft being inserted and beaten down after each horizontal row of knots.

In this way compact, sturdy rugs can be produced in less time than it would take by more conventional methods. It is extremely difficult to accomplish intricate, curvilinear designs using this technique, but, as traditional Tibetan designs are deceptively simple in conception, this is rarely a problem. This weaving method produces a distinctive ridge running horizontally along each row of knots at the back, which is clearly discernible and helps to distinguish Tibetan from Chinese rugs.

Pile materials in Tibetan rugs are wool, yak and camel hair. The wool is derived from two distinct types of sheep: a long-legged breed, mainly kept by nomads in the north, which is noted for the high content of hair in its fleece; and a short-legged variety kept predominantly by farmers in the valleys. A mixture of these two wools is normally used, and much of the natural lustre of Tibetan rugs is the result of the exceptionally high hair content of the wool. Yak and camel hair are employed mainly for flatweaves and blankets, but they can add additional lustre to the pile when used in rugs.

Natural dyes of certain types are common, though not exclusive, to Tibetan rugs; these are rhubarb (yellow), walnut (brown), and lac-dye (red), the Tibetan equivalent of cochineal, which is derived from the egg-sacks of a female insect (*coccus lacca*). They also use barberry (yellow), larch (greenish blue), polygonum (green) and safflower (orange), in addition to madder and indigo, and many of the other dyestuffs used in *Chinese* rugs.

Opposite: leaf meander border

Sizes and shapes

Most old and antique Chinese rugs are relatively small, rarely more than 6′ × 4′ (1.8 × 1.2 m), although larger items (especially Paotao rugs) can be found. Contemporary Chinese carpets, on the other hand, are produced in every conceivable size and shape, including runners, and circular, semi-circular and oval rugs. Each range of contemporary Chinese rug comes in a standard set of sizes, which often feature the same or very similar designs. Some ranges – the Standard Chinese, for example – progress from small mats to very large room-sized carpets; while others, such as Sinkiangs, may produce the same design in only two or three sizes. However, the Chinese weaving industry is infinitely flexible, and will produce any size of rug in any design, providing the customer is willing to wait. Authentic Tibetan rugs are rarely more than 6′ × 4′, but Nepali-Tibetan rugs are produced in larger sizes.

Measurements in contemporary Chinese rugs are usually expressed in imperial units (i.e. feet and inches), and the standard range of sizes is frequently produced to, more or less, the exact 'foot'– 6′ × 4′ and 9′ × 6′ (2.7 × 1.8 m), for example. Old and antique, and contemporary Tibetan items do not follow this practice, and may be expressed in either imperial or metric units, depending on the country in which they are being marketed.

Rugs for special purposes

These are not as common in China as they are in Persia (Iran), but there are some, mainly older rugs, that were made in specific sizes and shapes.

Pillar rugs were made to be wrapped around, or hung on, pillars, and are consequently long and narrow. They were usually made in pairs, and often feature dragons; these appear to be fragmented when the rug is laid on the floor, but when it is wrapped around a pillar, the bodies knit together to give the impression of dragons coiling around the pillar.

Saddle rugs (pls. 7, 8) were made throughout a vast region stretching from China proper into Mongolia, East Turkestan and Tibet to fit under saddles as protection for the horses' backs. They were woven for maximum durability, as they needed to withstand more than average wear and tear, and were also often used as seat covers.

K'ang rugs were made to fit on top of the traditional Chinese brick stove (*k'ang*), and measured somewhere between 4′ × 8′ (1.2 × 2.4 m) and 6′ × 9′ (1.8 × 2.7 m). Sometimes they were purely decorative, hiding the top of the stove and adding some colour to the room, but they also doubled as extremely warm and comfortable beds, particularly in winter. This was common amongst the predominantly nomadic cultures of Mongolia, East Turkestan, Manchuria and parts of Tibet, as well as the peasant Chinese, and is perhaps one reason why many traditional *Chinese* rugs evolved thicker, softer piles than their Persian counterparts. The exact purpose for which most old rugs were made is often impossible to ascertain, and almost any rug of the approximate size may be described as a *k'ang* rug.

Throne rugs were made as covers for thrones, or chairs, and are frequently scalloped, oval or rectangular with rounded edges, in order to fit the shape of the seat. These shapes are almost unique to the *Chinese* among older rugs, which perhaps explains why the modern Chinese weaving industry produces a wide range of oval, circular and semi-circular rugs.

Chapter III

Buying a Chinese rug

Oriental rugs generally represent extremely good value for money. Many low to medium grade items are often the same price, if not cheaper, than decent quality machine-made alternatives, and have the added advantage of retaining their value to a much higher degree. They are also far more flexible than fitted carpets, as they can be moved around, transferred to different rooms, or even a new house, radically altering the decorative tone without the need for major redecoration. In addition, oriental rugs possess the unique quality of being handmade; they are usually soundly constructed and durable, and even lower grade items normally give many years of service.

The decision to buy a *Chinese* rug – as opposed to a Persian or Turkish one, for example – should be based on a combination of an affinity with the general character of *Chinese* rugs, and whether or not they represent value for money in comparison with other rugs on the market at the time. (This second point is particularly important when considering the purchase of a Chinese rug in a Persian or other non-*Chinese* design.) However, one advantage that Chinese rugs have over rugs from other countries is their level of standardization and quality control; a prospective buyer can be certain that one 90-line Standard Chinese rug will, with very minor variations, be just as good as the next.

Decorative considerations

Most people buy contemporary *Chinese* rugs primarily to enhance the decorative impact of their homes, though any possible investment potential and long-term collectability may be seen as added bonuses. Consequently, the prime considerations – in addition to quality – are colour, design and size.

Colour
Contemporary *Chinese* rugs are made in almost every conceivable combination of colours, shades and tones. However, contemporary rug production is divided into several broad ranges, or styles (see p. 131), each with its own repertoire of colours and designs. It is therefore possible to experience some difficulty in finding a rug that combines the right colour scheme with the right design, although in practice, this is unlikely providing one has sufficient opportunity to shop around.
To create a harmonious effect, try to reflect the overall tonality of the room (pastel, rich,

sombre etc.), or ensure that at least one colour from the room is present in the rug. It need not be the dominant colour of either the rug or the room; better results are often obtained by matching subsidiary colours, or a dominant colour with a subsidiary one. For example, a predominantly blue rug with cream elements can blend perfectly in a cream room with no blues.
To create a contrasting effect, enliven the room by providing a vital counterpoint to the existing colours, taking care to ensure that the colours do not clash or cancel each other out. Contrasts often work best when the room is relatively neutral, with white or pale pastel walls allowing the strength of the rug to give the room its overall colour focus. A room can also be invigorated by the introduction of a rug with much richer shades of the room's dominant colour: for example, a pastel blue decor enlivened by a rug with richer shades of blue.
Pastel shades are extremely versatile and can complement most Western decorative

schemes, but care has to be taken with their placement, because they will show scuff marks and dirt more easily than deeper shades.

Rich shades are generally more suited to classic furnishings (dark-stained wooden furniture and richly patterned fabrics), but can also work with lighter furnishings, providing care is taken not to 'overpower' the rest of the room. Small rugs are rarely a problem, but large, room-sized carpets may prove too tonally intense.

Strong, dark or sombre shades are not common in contemporary Chinese rugs. However, some are found in most ranges (particularly Sinkiang and Antique Finish), as well as in many authentic Tibetan rugs. They find their best expression in rough-hewn 'farmhouse' or 'country cottage' settings, and can be equally at home in dens, studies, and rooms with relatively neutral or autumnal colour schemes.

Design

Design is generally less critical than colour, because almost any pattern can work if the rug's colours are compatible with the decor. Designs are, however, crucial to both the aesthetic integrity of the rug and its ability to reinforce the decorative atmosphere of a room.

Minimalist designs are common in the ranges of contemporary Chinese rugs that favour simple central and/or corner motifs set against a monochrome field. In some Nepalese-Tibetan rugs, in particular, the motifs are confined to the border of an otherwise totally monochrome, or variegated, field. These designs are especially suited to modern Scandinavian and Bauhaus-style furniture, and pastel or neutrally decorated rooms.

Curvilinear designs form the bulk of Chinese rugs in Persian and other, more traditionally Chinese, intricate designs. They often find their best expression in opulent or classically furnished surroundings, but can also add a degree of grandeur to a more simple decor.

Geometric designs are often at their best in rustic, Scandinavian and Bauhaus-inspired surroundings, but can also succeed in more classically furnished rooms, providing the colour schemes are compatible.

Repeating designs employ a single motif, or group of motifs, throughout the rug. The advantage of these schemes is that the pattern can be viewed from any angle, which gives considerable scope in the placement of the rug – an important consideration in locating runners and room-sized carpets.

Centralized designs employ a single central motif, or group of motifs, and are the most frequently encountered designs in *Chinese* rugs. Ideally, these rugs should be placed in a central position, with the furniture evenly distributed around them so as not to disturb the symmetry of the design. If this is not possible, try to allow roughly the same amount of space at each end of the rug by, for example, placing one side a few feet from the wall and the opposite side approximately the same distance from a large piece of furniture. This is especially critical with larger, room-sized items.

Vertical and horizontal designs, in which the design runs one way along the rug, can only be viewed properly from one direction; the most common examples in *Chinese* carpets are scenic or pictorial designs. Finding an ideal location is largely a matter of trial and error, but aim to place the rug where it cannot be seen upside-down (i.e. with the top end against a wall), or use it as a wall-hanging.

For more information on designs, see Chapter V (p. 97).

Size

Selecting the correct size of rug is not as simple as making sure that it fits into the available space. Rugs need room to breathe, and the stronger the design and colour scheme, the more space is needed to avoid them being cramped by the surrounding furnishings or overpowering everything else in the room. Similar care should be taken with runners, or rugs needed to fill a specific space; remember that doors may need to be opened across the rug, and that the length of the fringes is not usually included in the measurements.

Location and purpose

It is important to remember that certain types and styles of rug are more suited to some locations than others. A pastel-coloured, soft-pile rug may be ideal for a bedroom or little-used lounge, but unsuitable for rooms with heavy traffic or expo-sure to children. Durability is especially important in the case of runners and small rugs located near doors. Remember, too, that silk items, although very durable, show scuff marks and creases more easily than woollen rugs, and can melt when exposed to flames or intense direct heat.

Assessing quality

Assessing quality is not as difficult as it might first appear, and, with a little basic information and common sense, anyone should be able to distinguish between a good and a poor quality rug. There is, of course, some truth in the old maxim that 'you get what you pay for', but, as in other areas of commerce, price and quality are not always inextricably connected.

Quality is determined by a combination of a rug's appearance, the materials used, and how it was made. The former is a largely subjective area, but if you want to re-sell a rug, it is easier if the item coincides with popular tastes. More objective criteria can be applied to material and structural quality. The four main points to consider are: a) the fineness and regularity of the knotting, b) the clarity and permanence of the dyes, c) the texture and durability of the pile material; and d) whether the rug lies flat and evenly on the floor.

The first step in assessing quality is to *look at the back of the rug*. If it has a cloth backing, it is almost certainly 'hooked' or 'tufted' (p. 28), and cannot be considered an authentic hand-knotted oriental rug. In addition, the back of the rug shows the fineness and evenness of the knotting, and any damage or repairs that may not be visible from the front; this is especially important with older items.

Chinese rug grades are normally based on the fineness of the knotting, but it is important to remember that comparisons can only be made between rugs from the same range. For example, a 160-line Persian-design rug will normally be superior to a 120-line version from the same range; but it is not necessarily better than a 90-line Aubusson-design rug from the Standard Chinese range. In ranges that offer both open- and closed-back versions of the same style or design, the closed-back rugs are generally slightly better quality.

To assess the fineness of the knotting, calculate the knot-count (p. 26). A rough estimate can be obtained by seeing how close to the rug you can stand before the individual knots become clearly visible (similar to viewing an Impressionist or Pointillist painting); the closer you can get, the finer the knotting is likely to be.

Assessing the dyes is largely a matter of trust, both of your own initial impression of the rug's appearance, and the reputation of the particular type and grade. As a general rule, modern dyes are both attractive and permanent, and, providing the colours look good at the outset, the likelihood is that they will only improve with age. Equally, if the colours look dull and lacklustre, it is extremely unlikely that time will improve them. Contemporary Chinese rugs are made in workshops, and the colour irregularities (*abrashes*) that are acceptable in nomadic and village rugs should be treated as signs of inferior workmanship. The only exceptions to this rule are old and antique items, authentic (nomadic-style) Tibetan rugs and some of the Chinese Sinkiang range, which are based on more 'tribal' East Turkestan designs.

Assessing the pile material is again something that has to be taken largely on trust. As a rule, the higher the grade of rug, the more certain you can be that good quality pile materials have been used; the pile material in all contemporary *Chinese* rugs is generally good and should resist considerable wear and tear (p. 21). A simple test for wool is to fold or crease the rug, and see how soon the pile returns to its original shape; if it returns quickly, the wool has the necessary degree of springiness. Running your hands through the pile indicates the general health of the wool and it is a good sign if your fingers become a little greasy, as this shows the presence of natural lanolin. If the pile feels hard and dry, there is a danger that poor quality wool has been used or that chemical washing has removed the natural oils. Silk rugs should never be folded or creased, as this can damage the fibres. Look instead for suppleness in the fabric by brushing the pile with your fingers, and study the degree to which the colours change when viewed from different angles; the more intense the iridescence, the more likely it is that good quality silk has been used.

The length of the pile does not affect the quality of the rug, although it might be argued that $\frac{5}{8}''$ (16 mm) will take longer to wear down than a $\frac{3}{8}''$ (9.5 mm) pile. Some ranges (particularly the Standard Chinese) offer a choice of pile length in rugs of the same quality, but most ranges employ one standard pile length in all their grades.

Assessing whether a rug lies flat is a matter of placing the rug on the floor, then walking around and across it, until it has been viewed from every angle. Always use a flat and even surface, and try to look horizontally across the pile by lowering your eye-level to a few inches above the floor, as some ridges and troughs may not be visible from above. Then run your hands across the pile to detect any bumps. Unevenness of any kind is not acceptable in contemporary *Chinese* rugs (with the possible exception of nomadic- or peasant-style items), but, if minor, will not necessarily devalue old and antique items

Dating

Unless a rug's provenance has been systematically recorded, which is extremely rare, it is impossible to determine when exactly an undated rug was made; rival experts may fail to agree on the century of production, let alone the same fifty years. Even if the rug is dated, it is by no means certain that it was made at that time, because weavers often include the original date when copying older rugs. This is rarely a problem with contemporary copies, as even the most unscrupulous dealer would be unlikely to contemplate such an obvious fraud. However, there are a number of 19th-century copies of earlier rugs that could fool both collectors and dealers alike, and any rug dated to the first half of the 19th century or earlier should be examined very carefully before its attribution is accepted.

One should be especially wary if offered a Ning-Hsia rug from the Ch'ing Dynasty. Ning-Hsia rugs are generally regarded as the finest of the old Chinese, and those produced during the reigns of the Emperors K'ang Hsi and Ch'ien Lung are the finest, and therefore most expensive, of the fine (p. 119). Consequently, rug dealers (particularly in the Far East) have tended to attribute almost any early rug of uncertain pedigree to these periods. Proving or disproving such attributions is often impossible, and it is advisable to treat them all with scepticism, and judge each rug on its individual merits. Chemical analysis of the fibres and dyes, as well as structure and design, are helpful in establishing a reliable date and attribution, but even these are far from foolproof.

Age classification The Chinese carpet industry divides rugs into three broad categories: 'ancient' (pre-1911), 'old' (1911–37), and 'contemporary' (post-1937). However, in the West, anything made in the last thirty to forty years is generally considered 'contemporary', earlier this century 'old', and during the 19th century, or before, 'antique'. In this book the term 'old' has been used as a general description of rugs made during the 1920s or before.

The effect of age on colours can indicate when a rug was made, because exposure to light causes colours to fade. However, short exposure to strong light sources and chemical washing can produce the same effects, and one must be careful of assuming that a rug is old simply because its colours have begun to fade (pp. 23, 28).

What to pay

The two major considerations when deciding the amount you should pay are why you want the rug, and how much you can afford. If all you want is something that will give you adequate wear and tear in a busy corridor, for example, there is little point in buying an expensive silk runner, when a much cheaper woollen item would do the job just as well. This may sound self-evident, but it is easy to get carried away at an auction or succumb to a dealer's assurances of the wonderful 'investment potential' of more expensive items. Certainly, it is usually better to pay a little more for quality, but not at the risk of placing yourself in financial difficulty; especially as the lower grades of contemporary *Chinese* rugs should prove sufficiently durable for most purposes. Remember that rugs which represent extremely good value as furnishing items may not be suitable as long-term investments, while rugs with the highest investment potential may not satisfy the requirements of your home.

After deciding why you want a rug, the next step is to settle on the maximum you want to spend and then look at the range of items you can buy for this amount or less.

Price variations

A number of factors determine the price of a rug, including the cost of purchase in the country of origin, shipping, washing, import tariffs, exchange rates and tax. At any given time, most of these are relatively consistent throughout each importing country, and variations in the local retail price of almost identical rugs are usually due to the different overheads and profit margins of rival outlets, as well as to temporary surfeits or shortages of rugs, or a lack of sales in those markets. In addition, individual outlets may obtain batches of rugs at a special rate, or have them in stock before general price changes come into force. The variations in retail prices can be quite alarming, and it is not uncommon to find shops in the same town, or even the same street, asking 20% to 50% more or less for almost identical rugs.

Worldwide fluctuations in price are usually the result of an increase in the cost of production in the country of origin, or a decrease in the number of rugs being exported, and will affect all importing countries equally.

National fluctuations in price are usually due to the 'standard of living' in each country, and the difference in exchange rates and import tariffs between importing and exporting countries. Some countries, like the United States, operate a policy of favourable (low) tariffs on goods from countries with political regimes of which they approve, and unfavourable (high) tariffs on goods from countries with 'unacceptable' (mainly Communist) regimes. Consequently, the relative prices of *Chinese* rugs may be suddenly altered by dramatic changes in the diplomatic relationship between the countries concerned.

Do not forget that there are no recommended retail prices on *Chinese* or other oriental rugs, and dealers will normally charge whatever they think the market will bear. Therefore, *always shop around*, remembering that you can only compare like with like, and *never be afraid to negotiate*. Most retail outlets, with the possible exception of department stores, operate a reasonably flexible pricing structure, and the first figure they quote is rarely the lowest at which they will sell. The degree to which you can negotiate is determined by both the prevailing market conditions and your knowledge of the subject. Retail outlets need to recoup their costs and make a reasonable profit if they are to stay in business; consequently, there is always a limit below which they will not sell. However, it is not uncommon for most outlets to use a few 'loss leaders' (items sold at cost or below) in order to attract customers; and if any of these items are suitable for your requirements, you can obtain an exceptional bargain. Ideally, you should wait until market conditions are in your favour, or until someone is selling the rug you want as a 'loss leader', but in practice this is not always possible.

Therefore, research is vitally important, because the more you know about the subject, the better are your chances of obtaining a good quality rug at a reasonable price. Never be afraid to *take your time* making a choice; nor should you be reluctant to let it be known that you are considering buying at a rival outlet, as the fear of losing a sale to a competitor may have a favourable influence on the price.

Price and quality

These are closely connected in contemporary *Chinese* carpets, as there is a direct relationship between the cost of production and the quality of each item. A rug made to a 200-line standard will have roughly four times as many knots as a 100-line rug, and will therefore take that much longer to make; also, higher grade rugs frequently use better, and more expensive materials. This price/quality differential between grades (lines) is valid only for items within the same range; a 120-line Persian-design rug, for example, may be slightly more expensive than a 120-line rug from the Sinkiang range. There is nevertheless a relatively uniform relationship in the prices of all Chinese rugs, because the industry's systematic approach to production and quality control makes it possible to have standard costs for each specific range and grade.

The connection between price and quality is not quite as consistent in rugs from Nepal and other parts of the Chinese sphere of influence, because of their more fragmented, private-enterprise approach to weaving, but the same basic principle holds true: the better the rug, the more expensive it is likely to be.

Cost is also related to size, because wholesalers buy and sell rugs on the basis of a price per square foot (or metre), rather than per individual item. Therefore, as the wholesale price of all 90-line Standard Chinese rugs, for example, is more or less the same per square foot, a rug that is twice the size will cost twice as much.

In the case of old and antique items, rarity and collectability are often more critical in influencing price than quality or size.

Price categories

It is impossible to fix the prices of *Chinese* rugs in cash amounts because of constant local and international fluctuations in market forces; regardless of their accuracy at the time of writing, they would soon become out of date. However, the price of each range and grade of contemporary Chinese rug is relatively consistent in relation to any other. Consequently, if you know the price of a standard item, it is reasonably easy to calculate the average price of most other Chinese rugs. To a lesser degree, this holds true for items from other producing countries in the Chinese sphere of influence, as long as allowance is made for different exchange rates and tariffs, and for the more individualistic nature of their production.

If we take the most popular and widespread Chinese rug on the market (the 90-line, closed-back Standard Chinese) as our yardstick, it is possible to give a reasonable indication of the price of other ranges and grades of rug in terms of plus or minus 'x' per cent. A rug costing approximately the same would therefore be marked '0%'; one costing about 40% more would be '+40%', and one that cost 40% less, '−40%'. The price levels are based on the average wholesale cost, which (allowing for variations in import tariffs and exchange rates) is relatively consistent throughout the world. These price differentials do not, however, take into account local variations based on 'popularity' or 'supply and demand'. Similarly, the differentials between rugs made in China and those produced in Nepal or elsewhere, may be affected by the discrepancy in import tariffs and exchange rates, but these will not change the differentials between various grades and ranges from the same country. We can therefore say, making allowances for all the possible variables, that an 80-line closed-back Standard Chinese will be about 10 to 15% less (−10/15%), and a 150-line Persian-design rug approximately 50/60% more (+50/60%).

It is important to remember that price is directly related to size, so comparison should always be made by ft^2 or m^2.

Approximate price comparisons of contemporary Chinese rugs

Standard Chinese closed-back	wool	90-line	0%
Standard Chinese closed-back	wool	80-line	−10/15%
Standard Chinese closed-back	wool	70-line	−20/25%
Standard Chinese open-back	wool	90-line	−20/25%
Standard Chinese open-back	silk	120-line	+70/100%
Standard Chinese (tufted/hooked)	wool		−40/60%
Sinkiang with 'antique wash'	wool	110/120-line	+20/30%
Sinkiang without 'antique wash'	wool	110/120-line	0%
Antique Finish	wool	100/110-line	+10/15%
Persian-design	wool	110/120-line	+20/40%
Persian-design	wool	150/160-line	+50/70%
Persian-design	wool	180-line	+100/110%
Persian-design	wool	200/210-line	+130/150%
Persian-design	wool	240-line	+210/220%
Persian-design	wool	260-line	+240/260%
Persian-design	wool	300-line+	+270/+%
Persian-design	silk/wool	200-line	+200/220%
Persian-design	silk/wool	260-line	+270/290%
Persian-design	silk/wool	300-line	+300/320%
Persian-design	silk	260-line	+350/400%
Persian-design	silk	300-line	+450/500%
Persian-design	silk	360-line+	+550/+%
Persian-design	silk	400-line+	+600/+%
Tibetan-design (Chinese)	wool	50-line	−10/15%
Tibetan-design (Chinese)	wool	60-line	−5/0%
Tibetan-design (Chinese)	wool	80-line	0%
Tapestries	wool or silk	260-line+	+500/+%
Kelims	wool		−25/75%
Needlepoint (10-point)	wool		+5/10%
Petit point	wool		+30/40%
Nepalese/Tibetan (Kangri)	wool	50/70-line	+30/40%
Nepalese/Tibetan (Authentic)	wool	60/80-line	+50/70%
Indian/Tibetan	wool	50/70-line	−10/+10%
Bhutanese/Tibetan	wool	50/70-line	+25/50%

Old and antique rugs must be judged on an individual basis, and cannot be included in these comparisons.

Although it is impossible to compare the price of contemporary *Chinese* rugs with those from other producing countries, because of the variation in local costs, exchange rates and import tariffs, the Chinese range of 'Persian-design' rugs is sufficiently close to similar styles produced in Iran (Persia), India and Pakistan to make some comparison worthwhile. Remember that rugs employing almost identical designs may be produced in a wide variety of qualities, and you can only realistically compare a 260-line Persian-design Chinese with a rug of similar fineness (p. 26) from elsewhere. However, Chinese rugs in this range normally cost between 25% and 50% less than Persian equivalents, and are comparable with, or slightly cheaper than similar items from India and Pakistan.

Where and when to buy

There are several different types of retail outlet in most countries in the West, Far East and Australasia, each of which offers its own slight advantages and disadvantages to the prospective buyer. No one type of outlet has a monopoly on quality or value for money, and genuine bargains may be found in each, so always shop around. As in any other business, there is often a wide discrepancy in the knowledge, helpfulness and integrity displayed by individuals in every type of outlet; and, if you know and trust one particular dealer, you might be advised to stay with them, providing they have the right rug at the right price. Some retail outlets allow you to take a rug home for a few days so that you can see it in context; this is a precaution that cannot be recommended too strongly.

Remember that contemporary Chinese rugs are produced in different grades, and, although two rugs may look almost identical from the front, there can be a considerable gulf in quality and price between the two. Therefore always ask the outlet to tell you the grade (i.e. whether it is a 90-line closed-back or 90-line open-back, for example), as well as the type or range. Outright deception is rare, but less scrupulous dealers have been known 'imply', or fail to correct a buyer's assumption, that a rug belongs to a higher grade, or price bracket, than it actually does. Also, some shop assistants, particularly in department stores, make incorrect attributions due to their ignorance of the subject. However, every country has its own trading standards laws, and these also apply to the sale of rugs.

Specialist shops have the advantage of allowing you time to consider a number of rugs, both in the shop and often on a trial basis in your home. They also tend to have a wide selection of items in different sizes, designs and styles; and you can usually contact them should you experience any problems or require further advice. In addition, staff often have a reasonable understanding of the subject, which can be helpful if you are not sure exactly what you want. The main disadvantage of specialist shops is that they carry extensive stocks and are often located in prestigious locations, which means that relatively high overheads must be passed on to the customer.

Department stores offer many of the advantages of a specialist shop, frequently with the addition of credit facilities. However, with a few exceptions, they rarely carry an extensive range of items, and are usually unwilling to negotiate a price. The average store will probably have a fair selection of popular rugs, but unusual or top quality items tend only to be found in the more prestigious establishments. Some stores operate a franchise system, where the rug department is run by an independent dealer, and in this instance their pros and cons are the same as specialist shops.

Auctions are probably the most exciting and unpredictable method of buying a rug. Excellent bargains can be obtained, but unless you have some knowledge of the subject, you can just as easily pay too much. It is therefore essential to do your homework. Always check prices in the shops for similar items, and make an effort to familiarize yourself with the procedure and atmosphere of an auction. If possible, attend one or two beforehand, and never be afraid to ask for an explanation of the conditions before the auction begins. In particular, establish how the bidding is to be regulated, whether there are 'reserves' (a price below which a rug will not be sold) on any of the items or additional charges on top of the hammer price. It is usual for tax and, in some cases, a 'buyer's premium' (normally 10/15%) to be added; a rug bought on a bid of $200, for example, might therefore cost you as much as $250. Do not set too much store by the reasons put forward for the auction, because the dynamics are the same whether the sale is the result of a liquidation, a company trying to move its surplus stock, or private individuals selling their collections; the auctioneer will try to obtain the highest possible price for his clients, while the bidders endeavour to pay as little as possible for each rug. Consequently, your chances of getting a bargain are determined by both the interest shown in each item by rival bidders, and the auctioneer's (or vendor's) willingness to settle on reasonable reserves. You should be sceptical about claims of 'no reserves'; this may be true for some items, but auctioneers have a responsibility to their clients, and are unlikely to sell more valuable rugs for 10 or 20% of their usual cost.

The main advantage of auctions, apart from the opportunity of obtaining bargains, is that they are often the only means of buying locally for people living in provincial and rural areas. The main disadvantages are that you have to make an instant decision (although it is usual for auctioneers to arrange a viewing period prior to the auction), and full payment must be made at the end of the auction. Some auctioneers may be willing to change items if they prove to be the wrong size, colour or design, but this is entirely at their discretion, and much will depend on the specific instructions they have received from the vendor. If all the rugs are from one source, the auctioneer may be willing to exchange one item for another of similar price; but if the rugs belong to several vendors, exchanges may understandably prove problematic.

In most countries, auctioneers must abide by strict rules governing the conduct of auctions as well as more general trading regulations. Consequently, anyone buying at an auction will normally be protected by law if a rug should prove faulty or was sold under a false description (e.g. a tufted rug sold as a hand-knotted one). In practice, this kind of occurrence is extremely rare, although it is not unknown for an auctioneer to imply that a rug is more valuable than it actually is. With regard to old and antique items, it is important to remember that attributions of age and provenance are usually only 'opinions', and the auction house cannot be held liable for errors unless deliberate deception is intended.

Private sales are not usually covered by the laws that govern commercial sales, and, although specific regulations vary from country to country, the buyer generally has less legal protection. Private sales can still be worth considering, because bargains can be obtained. However, it is often a good idea to obtain a professional valuation, especially for more expensive items, as this will reassure both the buyer and the seller of a reasonable market price, avoiding the possibility of future recriminations. If the seller is a *private dealer*, standard trading regulations will normally apply, and you may well be asked to pay tax on the price. Private dealers can offer the same advantages as specialist shops, and may be able to locate unusual items, but unless you know them personally or by reputation you must take a chance on their reliability.

Catalogue and mail order services are useful for people who are unable to visit a retail outlet in person, but you cannot judge quality from a photograph, and this method of buying is not recommended unless there is a money-back guarantee.

Markets and antique shops can provide bargains, but finding a suitable rug is largely a matter of chance. Most non-specialist traders know little about the subject, so overcharging is just as likely as undercharging.

Foreign buying can be hazardous, and there is no guarantee that a rug will be cheaper in the country of origin, once import tariffs and shipping costs have been added, than it would be at home. Buying a rug as a memento of a visit to Nepal, Sikkim, Ladakh or Bhutan is fairly straightforward, but, unless you carry it with you, there is always a risk of its not arriving, or of your receiving a different, usually inferior, rug in its place. Also, most retail outlets charge 'tourist' prices (in Nepal shops generally adhere to government recommended prices), although hard bargaining or visiting more remote places may enable you to buy something for considerably less. Bureaucracy makes exporting from China itself difficult, and the regulations should be carefully studied before a purchase is made.

Buying rugs from other countries in the West is worth considering, as some items may be cheaper than they would be at home, although the additional costs of shipping and import tariffs should not be ignored. Remember that in some countries the import tariffs depend on where the item was bought, and in others, on where it was actually made. A US citizen buying a Chinese rug in Britain, for example, would have to pay the 'Chinese' import tariff, rather than the one applied to British goods. It is therefore important to ascertain, from your own customs department, which of these criteria apply before making a purchase.

Choosing the best time to buy Sometimes, the inconvenience of waiting for the best time to buy is more trouble than any financial saving might be worth. However, where possible, try to buy when supply is outstripping demand. A good indication of this is the number of sales, auctions and special offers in your area. The market can be further tested by visiting a number of retail outlets over a few weeks and noting the fluctuation in prices across a range of standard items.

Insuring rugs against damage and theft is always advisable. Less expensive items can be included on a general household policy, but separate cover is recommended for more expensive rugs. Keep photographs and descriptions of your rugs, and be sure to obtain a valuation when you buy or at a later date from an accredited valuer. In the case of more valuable rugs these can be lodged with your bank or solicitor. Remember that the insurance valuation is not the price you paid for the rug, but the cost of replacement, which, in practice, is usually more.

Selling a rug

Contemporary *Chinese* rugs do not have a high resale value, and are not recommended as short-term investments. Exceptional pieces (and possibly authentic Tibetan and more ethnic rugs) may prove to have long-term collectability, but the average contemporary item lacks the unique character that normally appeals to collectors. They are, however, attractive, durable and excellent value for money, and a market does exist, should you desire to sell after a few years. You are unlikely to recoup your initial outlay, but should be able to obtain a reasonable percentage of the purchase price.

Old and antique *Chinese* rugs are becoming increasingly sought after – despite being dismissed as 'inferior' by most auth-orities until the last quarter of this century – and, although they still do not quite command the prices of their *Persian* counterparts, they are fetching ever-larger sums.

Selling to a specialist shop is probably the simplest way to dispose of a rug, although they generally pay considerably less than the amount for which they hope to sell, and few will be interested in anything other than old and antique, and the more exceptional contemporary rugs. Older items are best sold through shops with specific experience of *Chinese* rugs. It is also worth exploring the possibility of a shop selling a rug on your behalf at a fixed percentage, rather than buying it from you directly. You will probably wait longer for your money, but may get considerably more.

Selling by auction is an option for both old and contemporary items. There is always an element of chance (particularly as rug dealers have been known to agree not to bid against each other in order artificially to deflate the price of certain items), but this can be largely offset by fixing a reasonable reserve (p. 40). Some auction houses charge the vendor – either a flat fee or a percentage of the hammer price; others cover their costs solely from the buyer's premium. Contemporary rugs are just as likely to attract buyers at a *general* auction as at one specializing in rugs. Old and antique items, in contrast, should only be sold through specialist auction houses, because they appeal mainly to a limited group of collectors.

Selling privately is often the best option in the case of contemporary items, although it is a good idea to obtain an independent valuation, even if only by visiting a few shops and finding out how much they are currently charging for your type, grade and size of rug.

Choosing the best time to sell is rarely critical with average contemporary items, and, if you need a quick sale, it is often better to accept a lower price, rather than hang on in the hope that the market will improve. However, with old and more expensive contemporary items it is usually advisable to wait for favourable market conditions, because of the potentially large fluctuations in the selling price, and to take the trouble to locate a suitable outlet.

Care and repair

Contemporary *Chinese* rugs have a justifiable reputation for durability, but they are not indestructible, and proper care and attention will enhance both the life and continued beauty of your rug. Wool is a marvellous rug-making material, but, in addition to normal wear and tear, central heating, air-conditioning and a number of household chemicals can have a detrimental effect on the fabric. A few simple precautions will ensure that your rug lasts for many years.

Correct underlay is extremely important, and you should never place a rug on an uncarpeted floor. An underlay (or padding) reduces the pressure, and subsequent damage, to the fibres caused by the constant squeezing between the soles of shoes and the floor. There are several underlays on the market, but probably the best general types are those made from solid sponge rubber – not to be confused with foam or ripple rubber, which are less suitable – and those made of jute and animal hair coated with rubber on both sides.

Cleaning should be done slowly and regularly, beginning by removing the surface dirt with a carpet sweeper or vacuum cleaner, preferably with beater bars. Always vacuum the back of the rug first, as this will ease the grit from the pile; then turn it over and run lightly across the front. Remember that vacuum cleaners with extremely violent beater bars may damage the foundation; if in doubt, use a carpet sweeper or brush. Old and expensive items, or those in a poor state of repair, should be cleaned professionally.

Shampooing should only be undertaken after the rug has been cleaned. Use a good quality wool (or silk) detergent, with perhaps a cup of diluted vinegar, and apply it gently and evenly across the entire surface of the rug; do not rub as this may cause the colours to run. The rug should then be carefully and systematically dried, preferably by leaving it out in the sun, and then checked to ensure that there are no pockets of damp in either the foundation or the pile; if there are, these can be removed using a hand-held hair-dryer. It is generally safer to employ a specialist cleaner when dealing with old, expensive or fragile items; but remember always to use a firm that specializes in oriental rugs, as the chemicals employed by many general cleaning companies for use on synthetic carpets can damage wool and silk. Shampooing extends a rug's life-expectancy, by putting back some of the natural moisture that is frequently destroyed in centrally heated or air-conditioned rooms.

Removing stains should be done by dabbing (do not rub) with the cleaning solution most suitable for removing the specific stain (coffee, ink, grease, etc.). There are a number of books that list these in detail (white wine, for example, poured immediately onto red wine considerably lessens the chances of a permanent stain). Remember always to use a cleaning agent that is compatible with the pile material, and never scrub or violently sponge a rug. When as much as possible of the discolouring substance has been removed, the area should be carefully dried. If the stain persists, or if the rug is valuable, it is advisable to consult a specialist cleaner.

Curling at the sides is common in tightly knotted rugs, and if uncorrected can cause uneven wear on the sides, which will undermine the appearance and value of your rug. This can be rectified by sewing (never gluing) a stiff PVC or fabric strip along the sides.

Repairs should be undertaken by professionals, particularly on older or more expensive rugs, although partially detached fringes or selvedges can be resewn by hand using matching-coloured wool or silk. Damage to the pile or foundation should be handled by a specialist.

Additional maintenance measures are needed to protect your rug from insect damage, extreme sunlight and uneven wear and tear. The former can be largely avoided by regular shampooing and using a compatible mothproofing agent. Long-term exposure to strong sunlight can cause excessive fading, which is especially undesirable if only part of the rug is usually exposed. This can be avoided by moving the rug at regular intervals or putting it in storage for the summer.

Before storing a rug, have it cleaned, shampooed and mothproofed; then cover both sides with polythene and roll it carefully with the nap – the way the pile faces – into a tight cylindrical form. Localized wear and tear can be avoided by occasionally moving or turning the rug, so that other areas of the pile are exposed to the normal day-to-day traffic. An additional safeguard is to make sure that houseplants are never placed directly on the floor near a rug, as this is the commonest cause of mildew (a type of fungus), which damages cotton foundations.

Wave border design derived from Chinese ink painting

Chapter IV

The cultural context

'The destinies of a people are shaped by their modes of thought, and their real history is therefore the history of their culture. The Chinese frame of mind has made the Chinese the people they are, and China the country it is.' This quotation is taken from the opening lines of Donald MacKenzie's fascinating book on Chinese and Japanese myths and legends (*China and Japan*, 1986), and while some historians may disagree with the finality of this statement, few would argue that the beliefs and cultural attitudes of a people are crucial factors in determining the way a country responds to differing internal and external pressures.

It is therefore important to examine not only the physical origins of the Chinese people, but also the religious, philosophical, social and cultural influences that have formed the Chinese 'character', and to see how these have in turn dictated the development of both China and the Chinese.

A brief history of China

Any history of China is more a record of the development of the Chinese people than a history of a specific country. It is easy to forget that the country we now call China only came into existence after the Second World War, and includes, within its current borders, previously independent nations and territories that were annexed or otherwise incorporated into the post-revolutionary state. In reality, modern China should be seen as an empire rather than a country – an empire that has systematically colonized the countries under its control and forced their inhabitants to adopt the Chinese culture and way of life (see pp. 11–13, 136).

Human development in China can be traced back to Peking Man, a discovery made in 1927 in a cave 30 miles (48 km) southwest of Peking (Beijing), which dates human settlement in China to the Palaeolithic period, some 350,000 years ago. This and subsequent discoveries suggest that the cradle of Chinese development focused on the area around the Yellow river (Huang Ho) and extended further into the Honan (Henan), Shantung (Shandong), and Shensi (Shaanxi) provinces of central and eastern China. Stone Age culture seems to have evolved 'primitive communes' (matriarchal, clan-orientated groups), which existed until the advent of the Shang Dynasty. Since then dynastic rule has been the norm, and a historical understanding of the Chinese is perhaps best achieved by examining the changes that took place during each dynasty.

The dynasties
The Shang or Yin Dynasty (*c.* 1766–*c.* 1122 BC) is the earliest period of Chinese history for which we have any definite historical material. We do not know whether the Shang were a separate ethnic group, or a sub-tribe or clan of an indigenous generic race, but there is no doubt that in terms of language and culture they were direct antecedents of the modern Chinese. The Shang rulers called themselves the 'Sons of Heaven', operated a slave- and property-owning society, and presided over religious cults that centred around human and animal sacrifices to ancestors and nature gods. Their territory extended south to the Yangtse river (Chang-Jiang), and west and north to the Shensi (Shaanxi) and Hopeh (Hebei) provinces. During their reign, a writing system and calendar were developed, and extremely fine ceramics, jade artefacts and bronzes were produced. *The Chou Dynasty* (*c.* 1122–*c.* 221 BC) began when the Chou (a subject tribe, clan or race

of unknown origin) defeated the Shang in battle. Their rulers continued to be recognized as the 'Sons of Heaven', but this appears to have been largely an honorary, possibly ritual, title which allowed them the trappings of power without the authority to exercise political control; the country was divided into numerous warring factions or states, which from the 8th to the 3rd century BC resulted in no overall ruler or influence over the disparate peoples who occupied the territories we now know as China.

This period did, however, give birth to Confucius (551–479 BC) and Lao Tzu (575–485 BC), the two most important figures in Chinese history, and the next three centuries also produced all the major schools of thought, with the exception of Buddhism and Communism, that have dominated Chinese culture ever since (p. 52). The later part of the Chou Dynasty, from c. 475 BC, is referred to by the Chinese as the 'Age of the Warring States'.

The Ch'in Dynasty (c. 221–c. 206 BC) brought unification to the warring states, and its most influential ruler, Shih Huang-ti, took the title 'First Sovereign Emperor', abolished feudalism, and began building the Great Wall of China. The territorial boundaries established by the Ch'in, which lie mainly east and south of the Great Wall, later became accepted as the indivisible area of China proper; and it is from the Ch'in and the area they controlled that the name 'China' is derived.

The Han Dynasty (c. 206 BC–AD 220) formed the first long-lasting regime that can be claimed to have had sole authority and control over China. It was during their rule that 'Mandarin'-style bureaucracy – based around powerful civil or military, semi-autonomous district or regional rulers – became established, only disappearing as the standard form of administration at the beginning of the 20th century.

Under the Han emperors, Confucian philosophy became the cornerstone of Chinese culture and social administration. Local officials were trained in Confucianism at provincial schools and imperial universities, and, aided by the invention of paper, went on to administer Chinese society according to Confucian ethics, modified to ensure the supremacy of the emperor and obedience to the state. It was also a period of advancement in art, mathematics, astronomy (water-clocks and sundials were in regular use), irrigation, and other developments which provided the basis for successive generations. Indian missionaries brought Mahayana Buddhism into China during the 1st century AD; Taoism was revived and slowly merged with popular superstition and folklore to produce the strange mixture of spiritual philosophy and primitive occultism that underpins so much of Chinese thought, even today.

No one can be certain of the exact ethnic relationship between the Han and the people of the former Ch'in, Chou and Shang dynasties. They may all have been merely different clans of the same ethnic group, or possibly a mixture of Mongol, Manchu or other racial origins, but there is no doubt that the Han Chinese are the direct racial antecedents of the modern Chinese; and it is now common practice to refer to the ethnic Chinese as the 'Han Chinese' in order to distinguish them from the other closely related racial groups.

The Sui Dynasty (c. 589–618) reunited China after the social fragmentation and warlordism that characterized the Six Dynasties (c. 221–589). Buddhism continued to integrate itself into Chinese culture and thought, and there were also significant developments in art, science and government administration, which laid the foundations for many of the achievements associated with the subsequent T'ang Dynasty.

The T'ang Dynasty (c. 618–c. 906) was a period of relative political stability and tremendous scientific and cultural development. The magnetic compass, the abacus, gunpowder and printing were invented or perfected, and, coupled with some remarkable medical innovations, including cataract surgery, helped to make China arguably the most technically advanced nation of the era. Religious tolerance and social change resulted in the establishment of a central government, the redistribution of land, improvement and extension of the canal system and the introduction of the

T'ang legal code; Confucian temples were built, and Buddhism developed into a vast and hugely influential institution. It was also a Golden Age of poetry, bequeathing us the works of the great poets Du Fu (712–70) and Li Po (701–62), and saw advancements in painting, ceramics and other artistic disciplines. During the T'ang Dynasty, Chinese art was strongly influenced by that of India and Persia, and a more elegant and realistic style began to permeate even the most traditional designs.

Much of this was due to the T'ang emperors' direct patronage, and their desire to make China the centre of culture and trade by operating an official 'open door' policy; this resulted in a constant stream of travellers, pilgrims, envoys, craftsmen, scholars and traders, coming to China along the Silk Route (p. 14). During this period China almost certainly came into contact with rugs, designs and weavers from Persia, India and the other rug-making countries along the Silk Route, as well as the nomadic cultures along its borders.

We do not know whether rugs were actually made in China at this time, but they were certainly imported, because the T'ang emperors had a taboo against leaving any part of the floor uncovered, and Buddhism (with over 40,000 shrines and 4600 temples recorded in a 9th-century document) provided a huge market for rugs of every size, quality and style. The poet Du Fu ended a poem addressed to his friend (an illustrious but poor scholar) with the lines: 'The fame of talent you have enjoyed for forty years, on the cold ground, you have no carpet to seat your guests.' It is not clear whether he is referring to a complete absence of floor covering, or whether he is making a distinction between cheap felt rugs (which had been in use for centuries) and authentic woollen- or silk-pile rugs. Very little is known about the quality and appearance of rugs in this period, but from contemporary paintings and writings they seem to have been primarily richly coloured, with fairly realistic floral, bird and animal motifs, set against intricate tendril and foliate forms, which appear to have been strongly influenced by Persian and Indian designs, and

contain little of the 'mystical' symbolism that dominates later works.

Towards the end of the T'ang Dynasty the Emperor Wuzong became concerned that the growing influence of Buddhism might threaten his power, and in c. 845 he ordered the destruction of Buddhist temples and shrines, and the enforced secularization of monks and nuns, on the pretext that Buddhism was a 'foreign' religion. Wuzong's attempt to eliminate Buddhism failed to achieve anything more than a temporary hiatus – it was by then too deeply entrenched in the Chinese consciousness to be so easily removed – but his actions broke with the spirit of the T'ang era, and, perhaps ironically, sixty years later it was the T'ang Dynasty itself that ceased to exist.

The Sung Dynasty (c. 960–c. 1279) restored relative peace and unity to the country, following a period of conflict and partition usually known as the Five Dynasties (c. 907–60). In some areas the progress of development begun by the T'angs continued. Paper money and credit notes were brought in to facilitate commerce, and the imperial house entered directly into trade, creating government monopolies which expropriated successful merchants and replaced them with over-bureaucratic, nepotistic and corrupt organizations. They also reversed the T'angs' 'open door' policy and adopted a more isolationist stance, discouraging contact with foreigners, and promoting only those things they saw as intrinsically 'Chinese'.

The Sung Dynasty is usually divided into the 'Pei' (Northern), and the 'Nan' (Southern). The Northern Sung, with its capital at Pien, lasted until c. 1127, when it could no longer defend its northern border against constant incursions by the Juchen (Manchu) tribes. The Southern Sung Dynasty dates from the removal of its capital to Lin-an in the south, from where it continued to rule over a reduced territory until c. 1279. In reality, however, the Sung emperors were never fully in charge of the whole of China, and, although they united much of China proper for long periods, other ethnic groups (such as the Khitan, Karakitai, Tangut and Juchen) always controlled some part of the country from their own capitals. Despite this, a number of advancements in agriculture, especially early-ripening rice and double harvests, meant a better chance of survival for the average person; the population, which had been relatively stable at around 50 million, doubled over the course of the next two hundred years.

Art and literature were consolidated, with native styles being revived, and certain art forms, especially painting, taking precedence over others. Some authorities argue that it was during this period that the Chinese intellect 'crystallized', and Chinese art took on the characteristics we associate with it today. The Sung were, however, unsympathetic to rug-making, and their second emperor, Taizong, refused to buy carpets for the newly built Longto Tianzhang pavilion, in Kaifeng, and ordered the removal of existing carpets from the Hall of Prolonged Happiness. It seems probable that they considered rugs to be 'foreign' and, as such, a corrupting influence on traditional Chinese arts and crafts. Rugs were also closely associated with the hostile nomadic cultures in the north, where rug-making continued to flourish, as the poet Lu You (*c.* 1125–1210) illustrates: 'Flickering I saw scarlet flames, the stove was burning in the morn, wrapped in a nomad's rug, violet wools are soft on the bed.'

The Yuan (Mongol) Dynasty (*c.* 1279– *c.* 1368) can be traced to the rise of Timujin (*c.* 1162–*c.* 1227), who reunited the warring Mongol tribes and, in *c.* 1206, was elected leader of the Mongol nation under the title Genghis Khan (Great Leader). He created the greatest fighting force since the Roman empire, and within a decade he controlled an area that stretched from the east coast of Asia to the Danube, and from the Siberian steppes to the Arabian Sea. The Mongol armies had reached 'the gates of Vienna' when they received news of Genghis Khan's death. According to Mongolian tradition, tribes must return to their homeland on the death of a Great Khan in order to elect a successor. Tradition was obeyed; and it is perhaps only this combination of custom and fate that prevented the 'Golden Hordes' from over-running Europe.

After the Great Khan's death the Mongol empire was divided among his various heirs. China devolved to his grandson Kublai Khan, who expanded its borders and founded a self-contained empire. He established his 'Court of Oriental Splendour' in the city of Cambulac, now Peking (Beijing), and re-opened the Silk Route as a major trading link, encouraging a constant flow of foreign merchants, craftsmen and advisers into China. Native prisoners and foreign captives with usable skills were set to work producing paintings, ceramics, sculptures and other arts and crafts, including rugs. Singers, dancers, actors, musicians, jugglers, concubines, astronomers, mathematicians and administrators were either bought or forced into imperial service, and for the first time in its history China established foreigners in positions of power. The Venetian Marco Polo (1256– 1323) spent seventeen years in Kublai Khan's service, before returning home with descriptions of the fabulous land of 'Cathay' which inspired generations of Western adventurers, merchants and writers.

Kublai Khan's 'open door' policy allowed important changes to take place in Chinese art and crafts: porcelain was introduced, and imported cobalt provided the glaze for the famous 'blue and white' pots. Kublai also re-established rug-making as a legitimate Chinese craft. Government-owned workshops were opened in Cambulac, and possibly other major cities, producing items of unparalleled sophistication and excellence – although it is not clear whether the weavers were native Chinese or brought in from other rug-making countries. Not surprisingly, as the Mongols were themselves a nomadic, rug-making culture, the Yuan Dynasty saw a development in the understanding of the different types of wool obtained from various breeds of sheep, and also from autumn and spring shearings. In addition to traditional nomadic weavings and the primitive felt rugs used by the peasant population, two distinct types of carpet, the patternless 'clipped wool' and the patterned 'downy', were produced, perhaps anticipating the modern concept of ranges and grades. Dyeing, using natural

A bamboo border design typical of the Ming Dynasty

pigments, also advanced to unprecedented levels, providing the basis for the later, wonderfully subtle *Chinese* palette.

Successive Yuan emperors followed Kublai's example and abandoned their spartan, warrior ancestry to pursue a life of luxury, continuing to build magnificent palaces, to import precious materials and artefacts, and sponsor the arts. A spirit of tolerance permeated much of Chinese life; not only could foreigners enjoy wealth and influence, but also, religious movements such as Islam and the previously suppressed Nestorian sect of Christianity were allowed to spread relatively unhindered. However, this tolerance did not extend to the native Han Chinese, or to the established Chinese institutions, which were vigorously repressed. It was probably this, coupled with the fact that the Mongols allowed 'soft living' to undermine their warrior instincts, that eventually led to the downfall of the Yuan Dynasty.

The Ming Dynasty (*c.* 1368–*c.* 1644) was established when a guerrilla army finally expelled the Mongols, and a Buddhist monk, Chu Yuan-chang, was installed on the Celestial (or Dragon) Throne, establishing his capital in the eastern city of Nanking (Nanjing). The dynasty that followed was one of mixed developments. Science and technological inventiveness declined, partly because bureaucratic stagnation continually undermined social efficiency and trade, but the visual arts and crafts reached a new peak of excellence, often surpassing the work of the Sung and T'ang dynasties; many of the paintings and ceramics of this period are without doubt some of the finest ever produced.

One of the first actions of the Ming rulers was to release the prisoner-craftsmen, who had been working as bonded slaves, and encourage them to use their skills in the wider commercial environment. This new-found freedom for both the prisoner-craftsmen, and the ethnic Chinese, who had spent nearly a hundred years under Mongol domination, seemed to inspire an explosion of creative energy, which resulted in a distillation of many of the technical and design advancements of the Yuan Dynasty. Painting, silk-weaving, enamelling, lacquering, bronze-casting and, perhaps most of all, ceramics reached even higher levels of technical and artistic sophistication.

The Ming emperors wielded absolute power and suppressed all criticism of their rule. They reversed the outward-looking stance of the Yuans, and reverted to an even more extreme version of the old isolationist policies of the Sung and Han dynasties. Anti-foreignism was rife, and European trade strictly controlled, operating, from *c.* 1557, as a virtual Portuguese monopoly through the port of Macau. In 1442 the Ming capital returned to Peking (Beijing), and some time later the building of the Forbidden City was begun: a city within a city – with massive courtyards, theatres, palaces, temples, treasure-houses, lobbies and residences, all enclosed by high walls – where the emperor could be as isolated from the rest of his capital as his capital was from the rest of China, and as China was from the rest of the world.

Surprisingly, perhaps, it is during this intensely xenophobic period that rug-making seems finally to have lost its 'foreign' stigma and become accepted as a legitimate, if minor, 'Chinese' craft. At the beginning of the Ming Dynasty, the vast majority, if not all, of the carpets in China were imported. A handbook of Chinese arts and crafts (the *Ko Ku Yao Lun*) published in 1387 defines these imported rugs as 'clipped velvet blankets', and goes on to say: 'They came from the western barbarian regions, and are made of wool' (an inferior material according to the Chinese). However, by the 15th and 16th centuries workshops in Ning-Hsia, Kansu and other parts of, mainly northern, China were flourishing, producing rugs with many of the characteristic colours (particularly blue), designs and symbolic motifs (e.g. *shou* and *fu*) associated with classic Chinese carpets.

The revitalization of Buddhism also created a huge market for rugs. The Stupa Temple, built in *c.* 1560 by the Tibetan Gelugpa Order (or Yellow Sect) at the site of their founder's (Lozangia ba) birthplace, about 50 miles (80 km) southwest of Sining in western China, illustrates the scale of the demand. Originally founded as a place to house Buddha's relics, it is divided into several halls, living quarters and ancillary buildings. One of these, the Sockchin Hall, had (according to contemporary records) its entire floor area of 21,300 ft^2 (1980 m^2) covered by prayer mats, its 168 pillars wrapped with silk pillar rugs (p. 31), and its numerous raised platforms decorated with pile weavings of different sizes and shapes. A small number of rugs in existence today are believed to have been made in the late Ming Dynasty, although their exact attribution is uncertain.

During the late 14th century, a crippled Turkoman chief, known as Timur-the-Lame, or Tamerlane (*c.* 1336–*c.* 1405), united Turkoman and Mongol armies and established an empire that stretched from his capital Samarkand, in Central Asia, through Persia and Iraq to Syria and Egypt. Having subjugated the western part of his empire, he turned eastwards and marched on China. His attempt to re-establish Mongol/Turkoman rule in China was thwarted by his death en route, but the threat of invasion hung over the Mings' increasingly despotic rule, and in *c.* 1644 the last Ming emperor, Ch'ung Chen, committed suicide when it seemed certain that he would be overthrown by rebels. One of his generals, in an act of extreme foolishness, appealed to the Manchus for help; the gates of the Great Wall were opened, and, once inside and the rebellion quashed, the Manchus seized the throne and established their own dynasty, thus ending the last ethnic Chinese dynasty to rule China.

The Ch'ing (Manchu) Dynasty (*c.* 1644–*c.* 1911) reversed the isolationist policies of the Mings and, internally, operated a system of social and cultural non-interference; apart from forcing the Chinese to braid their hair into pigtails (as a sign of loyalty, following an ancient Juchen/Manchu tradition), they made little attempt to impose their customs on the Chinese. They were also often passionate patrons of Chinese arts and crafts, and much of their two-hundred-and-fifty-year rule proved to be a time of relative peace, prosperity and artistic development.

The Manchus were predominantly a nomadic people of Tartar extraction, who added their rich rug-making tradition to that of China. The emperors K'ang-hsi (*c.* 1661–1722) and his grandson Ch'ien-lung (*c.* 1735–96), in particular, were enthusiastic patrons, ordering numerous rugs for imperial use. They were also supporters of Tibetan Buddhism (perhaps as a way of courting favour with the Mongolian and Tibetan minorities) and built thousands of temples, all of which needed rugs, thereby stimulating a huge second market for the growing rug-making industry.

In addition, many leading Manchu families preferred to lead their traditional nomadic lifestyle, pitching their tents outside the cities and spending much of their time hunting or engaging in military games, creating a third market for rugs. A fourth market emerged, among the more affluent Chinese, as it became fashionable to own carpets.

Consequently, rug-making flourished and diversified, and the traditional Chinese weaving groups (Ning-Hsia, Kansu, Paotao etc.) emerged fully as separate entities. In practice, these divisions between weaving groups were never totally consistent, and it was common for one group to produce rugs in a style associated with another if that was what the market demanded.

Nevertheless, a general pattern of regional characteristics emerged during the Ch'ing Dynasty that was as close as China had ever come to having clearly identifiable weaving groups; this pattern still forms the basis of our attribution of old and antique rugs, as well as many contemporary designs (Chapter VI).

Despite their general support of Chinese culture, the Manchus were nevertheless conscious of their racial identity, and openly discouraged intermarriage between Manchus and Chinese. However, this policy weakened during the course of their reign, and the various ethnic, religious and cultural divisions began to fuse into a more cohesive 'Chinese' identity. Nowhere is this more apparent than in rug-making, where the diverse influences of Turkoman, Mongol, Tibetan, Chinese, Persian and Indian weaving techniques and designs – allied with Buddhist, Taoist, Confucian, animistic and Islamic symbolism – evolved the unique characteristics that we now associate with Chinese rugs.

The Manchus' grip on power began to wane during the 19th century, as their identity became assimilated into that of the Han Chinese, and their policy of cooperation with foreign commercial interests opened the door to the disastrous Opium Wars (1839–42), after which China was forced to cede Hong Kong to Britain.

This was followed by the Taiping Rebellion (1851–64), the Sino-Japanese War (1894–5) and the anti-Christian, anti-foreigner Boxer Rebellion at the turn of the century, which brought European troops onto Chinese soil and heralded the fall of the Ch'ing Dynasty.

The 20th century
The pre-Communist era (*c.* 1912–*c.* 1949) began with the Republic declared by Sun Yat-Sen's National Party (the Kuomintang), in 1912, but it was not until a decade later that Chiang Kai-Shek succeeded, with Soviet and Chinese Communist support, in suppressing the regional warlords and achieving some degree of unification. After gaining power, he broke with the Communists – who retreated into the countryside, and formed their own army and government in internal exile – and then seized power. The Communists consolidated their support among the peasants and, after the Long March of 1934–5 (in which their forces retreated over 6000 miles (9655 km) into the remote northern Shensi province), emerged as a potent political force under the undisputed leadership of Mao Tse-Tung. In 1937 Japan invaded Manchuria, and the Communists joined with Chiang Kai-Shek and the Western allies against the Japanese until the end of the Second World War, whereupon they seized Japanese arms and challenged Chiang Kai-Shek's authority. Civil war raged for three years until Chiang's army was finally routed and forced to flee to Formosa (Taiwan) in 1949.

The Communist period began with the proclamation, on 1 October 1949, of the People's Republic of China. Mao Tse-Tung was elected chairman of the Communist Party and proved to be the prime mover in China's development until his death in 1976. In 1958 the Communist Party inaugurated the 'Great Leap Forward' (the 'commune movement'), aimed at bringing Chinese industry and agriculture up to the standards of the West, but it failed to bring about the desired results and caused a split in the Party between the 'radicals', who supported the scheme, and the 'moderates', who opposed such dramatic social change. Mao's final legacy to the Chinese people was the Cultural Revolution, which he hoped would rekindle revolutionary fervour and satisfy the increasingly

Stylized floral border typical of the Ch'ing Dynasty

vehement demands of the 'radicals'. The ensuing chaos and violence discredited the radicals, however, finally resulting in the 'Gang of Four' (led by Mao's widow) being arrested and brought to trial. The Cultural Revolution was officially declared a mistake for which Mao must take the blame, and in 1982 the more moderate vice-chairman of the Communist Party, Deng Xiaoping, steered the country through a new constitution which made a complete break with Maoism. The 'bamboo curtain' opened, and China made strenuous efforts to revitalize its trade and cultural links with the West.

A history of rug-making in China in the 20th century can be found in Chapter VII.

Chinese beliefs

Superstition and commerce

Despite growing interest in Chinese culture and art, the Chinese themselves remain something of an enigma. It is difficult to reconcile the apparent contradictions that seem to pervade everything 'Chinese'. On one hand, we perceive a highly sophisticated people, who are not only responsible for some of the world's most far-reaching technological innovations and profound philosophical thought, but also for an abundance of superbly crafted literature and art, as well as a medical system that is today drawing an increasing number of devotees; a people who respect their traditions, but who have adapted successfully to the commercial requirements of the modern world.

And yet if we look more closely at Chinese culture, we discover a superstitious people who seek advice from long-dead ancestors, call in geomancers to design their homes, practise numerous methods of divination, and cast spells 'to thwart enemies and bring good luck'; a people who believe in ghosts and demons, prophesies and charms, and who rarely doubt that favourable portents will ensure success, while unfavourable ones will bring ruin or death; a people who will work hard to achieve material prosperity, and then consider it well spent if it helps to appease ancestral spirits or preserve 'face' (personal honour and respect); a people whose aura of passivity, refinement and sophistication has to be tempered by the knowledge that thousands still flock to the public executions in modern China, and that emigrant Chinese communities throughout the world have brought with them the oldest criminal organizations in existence.

The Triads (or Tongs) as much as anything highlight the apparent dichotomy inherent in Chinese culture. They seem to have evolved from the same (or very similar) mystery cults (which flourished in the Middle East and elsewhere in early medieval times) as the Knights Templar and, in modified form, the Freemasons. There is a strong similarity between many of their essential rituals, which are based on the transition of the soul after death and include oaths of secrecy, esoteric codes of recognition and the importance of specific numbers (possibly based on the Kabbalah) in numerous rites. But while the Freemasons have evolved into a largely benevolent organization, the Triads are without doubt a criminal network, dealing in drugs, prostitution, gambling and protection, which preys on Chinese communities worldwide. They illustrate perfectly the strange mixture of the mystical and the mundane that permeates every facet of Chinese life: it would be hard to imagine Chicago, Berlin or London gangsters operating in a hierarchy that used titles such as 'Incense Master', 'White Paper Fan', 'Red Pole' and 'Straw Sandal' to indicate their position in the gang; nor could we envisage a group of French, Dutch or Italian criminals engaging in elaborate quasi-religious rituals before setting off to rob a security van.

Similarly, we would be shocked to discover that Swiss bankers consulted the *I-Ching* before making an investment, or that a New York stock-broker employed a *feng shui* geomancer (p. 103) to make sure that his office was designed in a way that would maximize favourable influences and keep pernicious (unprofitable) ones at bay. In Chinese communities, however, such behaviour is not only perfectly normal, it is also expected of anyone who hopes to succeed. When the Hongkong and Shanghai Bank moved their Hong Kong offices in 1981, a *feng shui* consultant was employed to ensure that the removal and re-installation of the famous lions that guarded the entrance did not attract any adverse *feng shui*. Similarly, it was perfectly acceptable for a young bank employee, Timothy Yau, to consult a *fu kay* practitioner (fortune-teller) in 1973, when the Hong Kong stock market was booming, to ask if the time was right for him to move into stock-broking. He was advised against the move; a few weeks later the market crashed, and Timothy Yau avoided financial ruin. These are just two of the thousands of similar stories that appear in Chinese newspapers every year, and they illustrate the strength of superstition and mysticism at every level of Chinese culture.

This dichotomy between the practical and the spiritual, the mystical and the mundane, is integral to what we might call the Chinese character. It permeates every facet of Chinese life and underpins the evolution, symbolism and production of Chinese rugs.

Philosophy and religion

Philosophy, rather than religion, has been the most potent force in providing the moral and spiritual basis of Chinese civilization. Confucian ethics, with their strong humanitarian bias, underpin much of Chinese thought, and both Taoism and Buddhism, although classified as religions, are based upon an understanding of spiritual laws and the evolution towards a more enlightened state of being, rather than the worship of a God and adherence to an immutable creed. In addition, many of the ancient animistic and shamanistic beliefs of the Shang Dynasty and before, with their emphasis on divination and the placating of ancestral and earth spirits, have been integrated, in a modified form, into all the major philosophical and religious movements, especially Taoism. This complex fusion of ideas has created a blend of superstition, mysticism, humanitarianism and logic that is uniquely Chinese.

Chinese mythology includes a number of creation myths, which generally follow the universal pattern of a union between the great natural deities (earth, sea, air, land) and the resultant birth of terrestrial life. Where Chinese mythology tends to diverge from the norm, however, is in its early introduction of an anthropomorphic trinity consisting of celestial beings, terrestrial spirits and human sovereigns, a cosmic triad that had divine dominion over planetary life. The Chinese term for this triad, *san-ts'ai* (which can be translated as heaven-earth-man), shows that even prior to the 2nd millennium BC the concept of 'God' as a perfected extension of man (a theme that would later emerge in Confucianism, Taoism and Buddhism) was already firmly established in Chinese consciousness.

There was also a widespread belief in the existence of spirits, both ancestral and those dwelling in trees, rocks, ponds and animals (animism). Success of both the individual and the group lay in the ability to consult and ascertain the will of these spirits through rituals conducted by holy men or women (shamanism).

Confucianism is the name given to a philosophical and social system based on the teachings of Confucius (the Latinized name of Kung Fo Tzu (*c.* 551–*c.* 479 BC), which became not only the cornerstone of Chinese thought until the Communnist revolution, but also strongly influenced the religious/philosophical systems of Japan, Korea, Vietnam and other countries of the Far East.

Confucius was essentially a teacher who felt he could bring a sense of order and morality to the confusion of the late Chou Dynasty under which he was born. He placed great stress on teaching by example, and constantly exhorted the emperor and other leading figures to conduct themselves in ways that would ensure they were perfect role models for their subjects. He also stressed the importance of courtesy; and argued that most, if not all conflicts, could be avoided if people followed strict codes of polite behaviour and showed the 'socially correct' degree of deference when meeting others, especially in public. Humanity, for Confucius, was innately good, and he believed passionately in the capacity of everyone, regardless of class, to improve their nature and evolve into the 'superior man' – a concept that predates, by over two thousands years, the German philosopher Friedrich Nietzsche's idea of the 'superman'. But, unlike Nietzsche, Confucius believed that the superior man must be motivated by love, compassion and the desire to be of service to others. One of his most famous sayings is: 'what one does not want to be done unto, do not unto others' – a sentiment that reappears five hundred years later in the teachings of Christ.

Concurrent with the belief that one should strive to become a 'superior man' is the concept of *jen*. It has been translated as love, benevolence and humanity, but can perhaps best be summed up by the Chinese ideograph for *jen*, which shows 'that which is common to two men' and carries with it the concept of the essence of humanity. (The five Confucian virtues are humanheartedness, righteousness, altruism, integrity and good faith.)

The two wings of Confucianism are represented by Mencius (*c.* 306–289 BC) and Hsun Tzu (*c.* 306–212 BC). The former shared Confucius' belief in the innate goodness of man and argued that there are four inborn seeds of goodness: *jen* (love, humanity), *yi* (righteousness), *li* (decorum) and *chih* (wisdom). He believed in the value of the common man, and is quoted as saying 'the people rank the highest, then the spirits of the land and the grain, and the ruler comes last'. Hsun Tzu, in contrast, argued that man was intrinsically evil, and could only be redeemed by accepting the admonition of wise teachers. Both agreed, however, that human perfection and sagehood were the ultimate goals of life.

Neo-Confucianism, which evolved in the 11th century AD, attempted to answer the questions arising from Buddhism and Taoism in Confucian terms.

Taoism, based on the teachings of Lao Tzu (*c.* 575–*c.* 485 BC) and Chuang Tzu (*c.* 369–*c.* 286 BC), is in many ways the complete antithesis of Confucianism. Whereas the latter appeals to worldly reformers and humanists, Taoism is the preserve of

The eight Taoist symbols

recluses who wish to withdraw from the 'illusion' of the material world. The word *Tao* can be translated into English as 'the way', and carries with it the same concept of a prescribed route or set of actions that must be followed in order to reach a particular goal.

In Taoism, the goal is *wu*, or non-being (the highest realm of existence), and the way to achieve this is to cultivate *wu-wei*, or non-doing (the highest ideal in the realm of conduct). The *Tao* is eternal, absolute, infinite and immutable; it is above 'being' and therefore cannot be described. A typical Taoist explanation of the *Tao* is: 'The *Tao* does nothing and yet there is nothing left undone.... When the road is straight I romp ahead, when the road twists and turns, I make the best I can.'

Taoism did not arise in isolation; many of its fundamental concepts were already deeply ingrained in the Chinese consciousness, and can be found in the classic works of Chinese literature that had been in existence for at least five hundred years before the birth of Lao Tzu. These were known as the Books of Changes, History, Poetry and Ceremonies, and they contained, among other concepts, the theories of the *ch'i* (life essence), the *yin* and *yang* (male and female polarities) and the *tai hsu* (Great Void). Taoism incorporated these themes into a system of spiritual advancement.

In its purest, most esoteric form the Taoist adept aims for union with the *tai hsu*, which will result in his sharing the immortal nature of the life-force itself. He achieves this by understanding and obeying the natural and cosmic laws, until he has shed himself of all worldly desires, ambitions and distractions, and reached the state of non-being (*wu*), where he is at one with the *Tao*. This is the secret alchemy of Taoism: the process of turning something that is flawed and mortal into something perfect and eternal. But just as Western alchemy was deflected from its spiritual roots (changing base men into spiritually pure men) to more worldly objectives (turning lead into gold) so, too, Taoist alchemy became associated with the search for longevity and eternal life.

Similarly, the concepts of the *ch'i* and the *yin* and *yang* have found their greatest expression in Chinese medicine; and the Taoist belief in a 'spirit of life' that infuses all of nature merged with the ancient animistic doctrine that animals, birds, plants and objects are imbued with the power to impart qualities (strength, love, wisdom, etc.) and alter fate. Consequently, fortune-telling and divination, which in reality originate from the ancient shamanistic cults of the Shang Dynasty, can point to numerous Taoist aphorisms as 'spiritual' authority for their practice: for example, 'To know the outcome, look to the root. . . . Study the past to know the future. . . . Know one part of the whole, and you know the whole.'

This holistic view of the universe is at the root of Chinese symbolism and art, not only in the use of animals, birds, plants and objects to evoke 'sympathetic magic', but also in the way the spatial relationship between different elements (harmonizing the *yin* and *yang*, for example, p. 113) and the invisible natural 'energy lines' (dragon veins, p. 101) are incorporated into paintings and designs. (See also p. 114.)

Buddhism was founded by the Hindu prince Siddhartha Gautama (*c.* 567–487 BC), who came to be known as the Buddha, or 'Enlightened One'; he was reputed to have become so disillusioned with the suffering he saw around him, and the inability, even in death, to escape from the inevitable sorrow of the 'cycle of lives' (reincarnation), that he left his palace and his family to become a mendicant and ascetic. After six years of study and self-deprivation, despairing of ever finding a solution, he sat under a Bo tree, and the answers to his questions suddenly became clear. These are enshrined in the 'four noble truths': 1) existence is unhappiness; 2) unhappiness is caused by selfish desires and cravings; 3) desire can be destroyed; and 4) the way to destroy desire is to follow the 'eight-fold path', whose steps are right thinking (clarity and focus of thought); right speaking (truth); right conduct (including abstinence from immorality and taking life); right livelihood (engaging only in employment that will not cause anyone suffering or harm); right effort (constantly striving for improvement); right awareness (understanding the link between the past, present and future); and right contemplation and meditation.

In essence, Buddhism seeks to transcend the suffering inherent in life, both for oneself and others, by a combination of correct behaviour and thought, coupled with meditation and spiritual exercises. Buddha neither affirmed nor denied the existence of a God; he simply ignored the question as one that could not, and need not, be answered. He saw the goal of all humans as being to develop their 'Buddha Nature' and thereby achieve *nirvana* (salvation from the cycle of lives).

Buddhism spread slowly from India during the 1st millennium AD, and by the 10th century it was firmly entrenched in the cultural and religious life of China, Tibet,

The eight Buddhist symbols

its inter-reaction with the native Chinese belief systems it evolved into *Ch'an* Buddhism (which is traditionally traced back to the legendary 'smile' exchanged between the Buddha and his disciple Mahakasyapa). It was exported to Japan around the 5th and 6th centuries AD, where, as Zen, it has continued to flourish.

The essence of *Ch'an* is that the mind should be purged of all distractions and distortions and kept clear and pure, so as to glimpse the 'fleeting truth' of reality and achieve one's own Buddha Nature. *Ch'an* differs from other branches of Buddhism in its emphasis on meditation and the use of techniques that include 'teaching without words' and 'pointing directly to the mind'. It also employs parables and *koans* (unsolvable riddles) to teach the futility of seeking intellectual answers to spiritual questions, and places great stress on acting spontaneously, without self-consciousness or hesitation. This latter quality appealed to the 'warrior classes' in both China and Japan, and provided the philosophical basis for the *Bushido* (the Samurai code) and many of the Eastern martial arts. It was also influenced by many of the same animistic and shamanistic elements of Chinese culture that had merged with Taoism, resulting in a rich and visually exciting extension of Buddhist mythology.

Tibetan Buddhism is the result of a fusion between Mahayana Buddhism and the shamanistic Tibetan religion, Bon. It also incorporates the rigid monastic practices of early Theravada (Hinayana) Buddhism, the intellectual disciplines of Madhyamika and Yogacara philosophy and many of the rituals of the Vajrayana (Tantric) Buddhists. What sets Tibetan Buddhism apart, however, is the belief in a cycle of reincarnated 'lamas', born with spiritual and temporal authority over Tibet. It also contains a vast pantheon of divine beings (each with its own family and consorts, who have contrasting benevolent and terrifying aspects); these are considered by the religiously sophisticated to be symbolic representations of psychic forces, but are taken as literal and living realities by the population at large.

Nepal, Mongolia, Ceylon (Sri Lanka), Burma, Siam (Thailand), Japan and other parts of Indo-China. During the first thousand years, it split into several branches or schools of thought, some of which proved more popular in certain countries than others, and underwent further modifications as it came into contact with existing native beliefs. (See also p. 114.)

Chinese Buddhism is predominantly Mahayana Buddhism (believed to have been imported into China some time between AD *c.* 516 and 534 by the Indian monk Bodhidharma) with a strong Taoist and, to a lesser degree, Confucian accent. Several changes were made to the original Buddhist doctrines, including the reinterpretation of the Sanskrit word *nirvana* from its original meaning of 'extinction' to the more acceptable 'perfection'. Through

Buddhism was brought back to Tibet during the 7th to 10th centuries by a succession of teachers and monks, of whom the Tantric master Padmasambhava and the Mahayana scholar Santiraksita were the most famous. In *c.* 1042 the great teacher Atisa arrived from India and initiated a reform movement that led to the Gelugpa (or 'One of the Virtuous System') sect; this, in turn, evolved into the order of the Dalai and Panchen Lamas, who eventually ruled the spiritual and temporal life of the Tibetan people until the country was annexed by China in 1950. The religious devotion of the Tibetan people is illustrated by the fact that not only was every available piece of Buddhist literature translated into Tibetan, but also that many of the original Sanskrit (Indian) texts are now only available in their Tibetan translations. In addition, there is a fascinating legacy of mythology and symbolism arising from the fusion of separate schools of Buddhism with the indigenous Bon religion.

Other philosophical systems arising under the late Chou Dynasty included *Moism*, founded by Mo Tzu (*c.* 470–*c.* 391 BC), which advocated a doctrine of universal love.

Moists believed in the Confucian idea of *jen*, and also in 'following the will of heaven' and motivating group actions by identification with a superior leader or cause. Moism was revived in the mid-20th century, with Mao Tse-Tung as the focus.

Legalism held that humans were essentially evil, and advocated a system of cynical political thought similar to that put forward over fifteen hundred years later by the Italian Renaissance thinker Niccolò Machiavelli, in his treatise *The Prince*.

The School of Logicians, founded by Hui Shih, Kung-sun Lung Tzu and other 'Name Philosophers' (*Ming Chia*), reacted against the predominantly esoteric teachings of the era by advocating a more detached approach to finding truth.

The School of Diviners sought to develop the theories of the *yin* and *yang* and the 'five elements' (metal, wood, water, fire and earth) into a broader cosmology and explanation of the universe. Their work was largely absorbed into other philosophical and religious systems, mainly Taoism, and has become closely associated with astrology, alchemy, occultism and, perhaps most influentially, Chinese medicine.

Note: In the colour plates section the country of origin of each rug is given in Roman type.
Other countries where similar rugs are produced are in italic.
For a detailed explanation of the designs, see Chapter V.

1. **OLD CHINESE** (Peking?) with masks, stag and deer motifs, and Buddhist and Taoist symbols (China)

2. **OLD CHINESE** imperial dragon rug with wave and cloud border (China)

3. **OLD CHINESE** (Ning-Hsia) 'two-seat' temple rug with fo-dog motifs (China/*Tibet*)

4. **OLD CHINESE** (Kansu?) with fret medallion-and-corner design (China)

5. **OLD CHINESE** 'Peking' with allover shou, butterfly and peony design (China)

6. **OLD CHINESE** 'Suiyuan' with fret medallion, and cloud and 'endless knot' field motifs (China)

7. **OLD CHINESE** (Kansu?) saddle rug with fret and floral medallion,
and cloudband border (China/*Tibet/Mongolia*)
8. **OLD CHINESE** (Kansu?) saddle rug with shou and 'endless knot' motifs (China/*Tibet/Mongolia*)

9. **CONTEMPORARY CHINESE** 'Sinkiang range', based on old East Turkestan
ay-gul scheme (China)

10. **CONTEMPORARY CHINESE** 'Sinkiang range' based on an old East Turkestan
pomegranate design (China)

11. **OLD CHINESE** 'Peking' with mixed floral medallion (China)

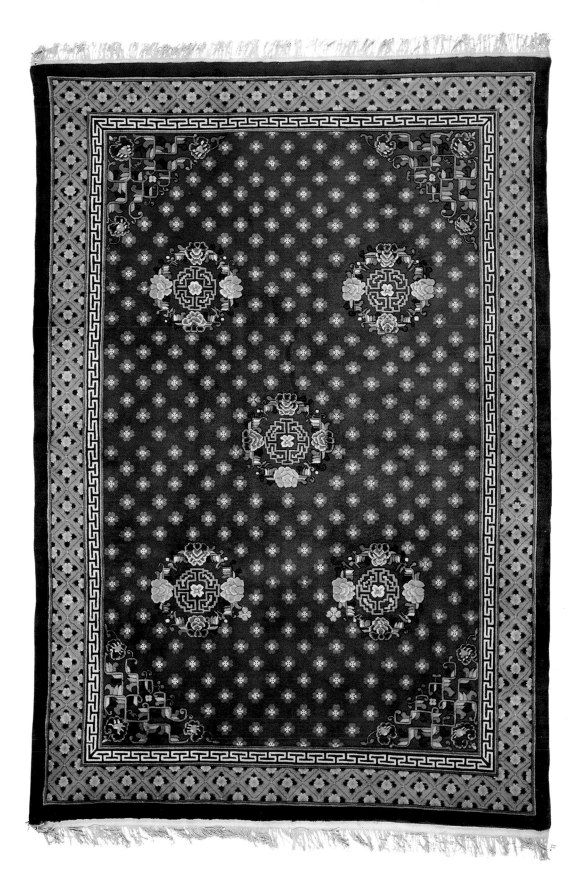

12. **CONTEMPORARY CHINESE** 'Antique Finish range' (Peking) with shou and floral motifs (China)

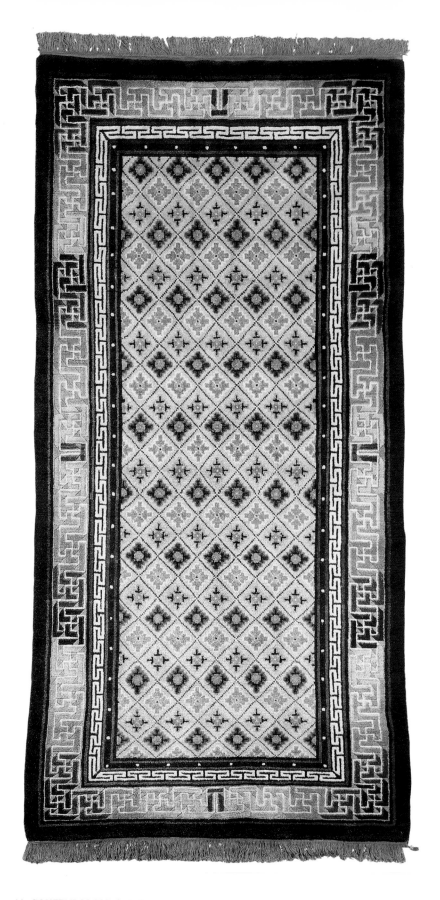

13. **CONTEMPORARY CHINESE** 'Antique Finish range' with diagonal lattice design (China)

14. **CONTEMPORARY CHINESE** 'Antique Finish range' (Peking) combining fret and floral motifs (China)

15. **EARLY CONTEMPORARY CHINESE** 'Peking range' with dragon medallion (China)

16. **CONTEMPORARY** 'Standard Chinese range' with dragon medallion (China)

17. **CONTEMPORARY** 'Standard Chinese range' silk, with Western-inspired peony design (China)

18. **CONTEMPORARY** 'Standard Chinese range' silk with Western-inspired floral design (China)

19. **CONTEMPORARY CHINESE** 'Kelim range', Westernized floral design (China)

20. **CONTEMPORARY CHINESE** 'Needlepoint range', Westernized floral design (China)

21. **CONTEMPORARY** 'Standard Chinese' circular rug with Aubusson design (China)
22. **EARLY CONTEMPORARY CHINESE** 'Peking range', with floral and shou medallion (China)

23. **CONTEMPORARY NEPALI/TIBETAN** rug with Westernized Tibetan medallion design (Nepal)

24. **CONTEMPORARY CHINESE** 'Persian-design range' with allover Shah Abbas scheme (China)

25. **CONTEMPORARY NEPALI/TIBETAN** rug with Western Art Nouveau design (Nepal)

26. **CONTEMPORARY CHINESE** 'Tibetan range' with cloud and shou allover design (China/*Nepal*)

27. **CONTEMPORARY NEPALI/TIBETAN** chessboard design (Nepal)

28. **CONTEMPORARY AUTHENTIC TIBETAN**, with allover peony design (Nepal/*India*)

29. **CONTEMPORARY AUTHENTIC TIBETAN**, triple peony design (Nepal/*India*)

30. **CONTEMPORARY AUTHENTIC TIBETAN** with triple fret medallion (Nepal/*India*)

31. **CONTEMPORARY AUTHENTIC TIBETAN** with fighting phoenixes (Nepal/*India*/*Bhutan*)

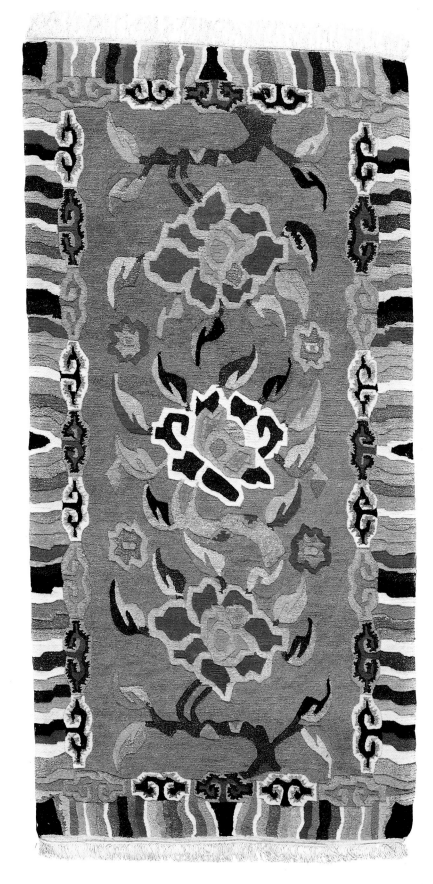

32. **CONTEMPORARY AUTHENTIC TIBETAN**, triple peony design
with cloud and wave border (Nepal/*India*)

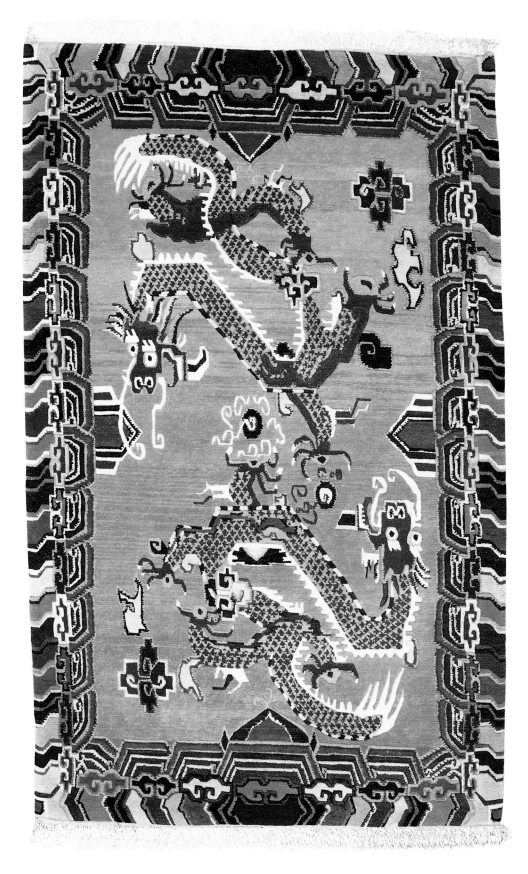

33. **CONTEMPORARY AUTHENTIC TIBETAN**, with fighting dragons and cloud,
wave and mountain border (Nepal/*Bhutan*/*India*)

34. **CONTEMPORARY NEPALI/TIBETAN** Tiger rug (Nepal)

35. **CONTEMPORARY AUTHENTIC TIBETAN** Tiger rug (Nepal)

36. **CONTEMPORARY AUTHENTIC TIBETAN** Tiger rug (Nepal)

37. **CONTEMPORARY AUTHENTIC TIBETAN** nomadic-style rug made from undyed wool (*Nepal/India*)

38. **CONTEMPORARY AUTHENTIC TIBETAN** with lions/fo-dogs, mountain and cloud border (Nepal)

39. **CONTEMPORARY AUTHENTIC TIBETAN** snow leopard design (Nepal)

40. **CONTEMPORARY CHINESE** 'Tapestry range', with cranes (China)

41. **CONTEMPORARY CHINESE** 'Tapestry range', mythological scene (China)

42. **OLD CHINESE** (Paotao?) scene from a folk tale featuring the monkey god (China/*Tibet*)

Chapter V

Designs

Chinese designs are significantly different from those of the other rug-producing countries, both in their general appearance and in the religious, cultural and artistic influences that underpin them. The most obvious reason for this is that Islam – the dominant influence in most weaving countries – made little impact on China; although there is a small minority of Chinese Muslims (*Hui Hui*), they played little part in the evolution of rug-making in China. Consequently, the artistic and symbolic traditions of Islam barely penetrated beyond the outlying areas of Mongolia and East Turkestan; and even in these areas, the more overtly 'Islamic' Turkoman designs were modified by non-Islamic, Chinese influences to the point where it is now extremely difficult to say, for example, whether the central disk-like motifs that are common in these rugs were originally *Persian/Islamic* medallions, with their heraldic or mosque-dome symbolism, or *Chinese/Buddhist/Taoist* mandalas illustrating the 'wheel of life' (p. 106).

Chinese designs diverge from *Persian/Islamic* ones in two other important ways: first they draw widely on other art forms (painting, ceramics, etc.) for their themes; and second, the motifs are often used to create a visual talisman, or iconograph, which is aimed at warding off evil influences, and bestowing good fortune and a variety of desirable personal qualities on the owner.

Belief in the power of symbols is central to Chinese culture, and even today most people try to surround themselves with symbols that they hope will improve their fortunes. Contemporary rug designs are therefore not only a matter of aesthetics, offering historical insight into ancient superstitions and beliefs; they are also part of the ongoing reality of Chinese life. A Chinese businessman may buy a rug with a certain design simply because he finds it visually attractive, but his choice is frequently influenced by the symbolic meaning of the motifs.

The fundamentals of Chinese rug design

Contemporary *Chinese* rug designs can be traced to five main sources. The first three – which could be defined as: a) mythological and religious sources (Taoism, Buddhism), b) other art forms (painting, ceramics, embroidery), and c) weaving groups from the wider Chinese sphere of influence (East Turkestan, Mongolia) – can be described as essentially *Chinese*.

In addition, China now produces a range of rugs based exclusively on traditional Persian designs, which are faithful copies of the originals and have no connection with China other than the fact that they were made there (pl. 24). Similarly, China has been producing rugs based on European and North American designs for most of the

20th century, and, ironically, these are the types of design most Westerners usually associate with typical Chinese rugs (pls. 17, 18, 21).

Some ranges of contemporary rugs (e.g. the Persian-design and Sinkiang) are based almost exclusively on one of these five sources, but most combine designs and motifs from a number of origins. For example, the Standard Chinese range produces designs drawn from other art forms (landscapes), religious and mythological sources (dragon themes), as well as essentially Western compositions (Aubusson, certain floral schemes) and those from East Turkestan, Tibetan and other traditional *Chinese* weaving groups. Some rug compositions are drawn exclusively from one source, but the vast majority combine elements from two or more: for example, a predominantly 'landscape', or Aubusson scheme with *shou* motifs employed in the border.

In old and antique items, some specific designs are closely associated with individual regions or weaving groups (the 'pomegranate' pattern, for example, is primarily found in East Turkestan rugs); others (medallion/mandala schemes) appear, with minor tonal and thematic changes, in rugs from several different regions and groups. Similarly, some contemporary rug ranges favour specific designs either because they have a natural affinity with the theme of that particular range (for example, Shah Abbas and prayer-rug schemes in the Persian-design range), or alternatively because they are compatible with the overall physical structure of the range (knot-count, pile length etc.). For example, bolder, less intricate, Western-inspired schemes are suitable for rugs in the less finely knotted Standard Chinese range (pls. 16–18, 21).

Identifying *Chinese* rugs by their designs can be extremely difficult, because almost identical designs can be found in items from different weaving groups or ranges. This is true to some degree with both contemporary and older items, although older rugs are often attributed, with varying degrees of certainty, to specific weaving groups because their designs are similar to those associated with rug-production in the region (see Chapter VI).

In contemporary rugs, however, design is a useful indication of the range to which a rug belongs, because each range is normally limited to its own broad repertoire of designs. The first step is to eliminate the ranges to which a rug is unlikely to belong. For example, if we know that 'pomegranate' designs are almost exclusive to the 'Persian-design' and 'Sinkiang' ranges (p. 132), we can effectively eliminate all the other ranges, and then use our knowledge of colour schemes and structural factors (e.g. knot-count, pile length, type of wash) to choose between the two.

Exactly the same process is used for attributing rugs that employ designs used in more than one range: for example, the Standard Chinese, Antique Finish and Tapestry ranges all employ traditional Chinese landscape designs, but their structure and colouring is sufficiently different to allow for relatively easy attribution. If the scheme is found on a pastel-coloured rug with a low knot-count and thick pile, it almost certainly belongs to the Standard Chinese range. However, if the rug is very finely knotted, with a low pile and rich colouring, it is most probably a tapestry; if it is less finely knotted and intense in colour, but has a short pile, it is more likely to belong to the Antique Finish range.

For fuller details of the designs used by the different ranges of contemporary rugs, and traditional weaving groups associated with old and antique items, see the following sections, and Chapters VI and VII.

The anatomy of a rug
Medallion, or mandala (A) Any large central motif, usually round or spherical, employed

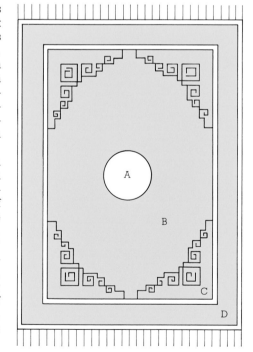

as the focal point of the design (p. 106, and pls. 1, 3, 16, 22 etc.).

Field (B) The main area of the rug within the borders.

Spandrels (or corners) (C) The four right-angled areas where the field meets the inner border – frequently containing motifs that echo the central medallion, if one is used (e.g. pls. 15, 16). In some *Chinese* rugs, the spandrels contain the only motifs on the field.

Main border (D) The largest, and often the central or only border. It usually contains its own motifs and subsidiary designs.

Minor borders Smaller, supplementary borders, normally arranged in equal numbers on either side of the main border.

Ground The underlying, or background, colour in any part of the rug (e.g. a cream-ground border), sometimes used as an alternative for the field.

Motif Any single form or cohesive combination of forms (e.g. a bouquet of flowers) used as an element in the design.

Open field A monochrome field, with either no decoration at all or only a few, widely spaced motifs. It is often used in medallion/mandala schemes (e.g. pls. 15, 37).

Variegated field One in which an allover or repeating design continues unchanged over different-coloured grounds.

Palette (or dyer's palette) Term used to describe the overall colour scheme (e.g. a rich or pastel palette).

Patina The surface gloss, or sheen, of the pile (e.g. a silky or dull patina).

Basic design formats

Allover designs Those in which the entire field is covered by the same pattern (pl. 21).

Repeating designs employ a single motif, or group of motifs, which is uniformly repeated over the field (pls. 5, 26).

Panelled designs Those in which the field has been divided into panels, or segments (pl. 25), which usually contain alternating coloured grounds or motifs.

Pictorial designs are those that employ a recognizable scene drawn from nature, mythology or life. It is not enough simply to portray naturalistic forms (e.g. garlands of flowers); they must also be set in the context of a wider environment, such as a landscape, group of figures or mythological scene. Pictorial designs are the predominant theme of contemporary tapestries (pls. 40, 41), and are used to a lesser extent in items from the Standard Chinese, Antique Finish and Persian-design ranges. In old and antique rugs they are found mainly in Paotao rugs (pl. 42), and sometimes in those attributed to Ning-Hsia and Suiyuan. They can also appear occasionally in most other old *Chinese* rugs, especially Tibetan (pl. 39), but are extremely rare in items from Mongolia and East Turkestan.

Prayer-rug designs are based on the physical structure of the mosque. The top of the composition is usually an arch (the *mihrab*, where the *qibla*, or sacred stone, is kept, and which devotees face when praying); the bottom is a rectangular area, known as the prayer field, representing the 'clean spot' on which Muslims have to kneel during prayer. In contemporary Chinese weaving, prayer-rug designs are normally found only in items from the Sinkiang and Persian-design ranges. In old and antique items, this design is almost exclusively confined to East Turkestan and Mongolian rugs.

Saph designs Essentially multiple prayer-rug schemes, where two or more self-contained prayer-rug formats run side by side along the length of the rug. This scheme is confined to the same weaving groups and ranges as prayer-rug designs, but is considerably less common.

Tree-of-Life designs employ a central trunk-like form, with branches sprouting from either side, usually as an allover pattern through the length of the rug. The Tree of Life is one of the oldest and most universal symbols, and usually represents some link between the world of men and the worlds beyond. Its most popular manifestation in *Chinese* rugs, the 'pomegranate' scheme (pl. 10), is normally only found in the same ranges and groups of carpets as prayer-rug designs.

Gul designs, the foundation of nearly all Turkoman compositions, usually consist of one or two types of *gul* (lozenge-shaped motifs) repeated in an allover format. The term *gul* is believed to derive from either a Persian word for 'flower', or, perhaps more aptly, an ancient Turkish word meaning 'clan'. Many authorities now lean more towards the latter theory, because the Turkoman nomads have used the *gul* motif as a tribal emblem, or standard, for centuries. Each tribe traditionally had its own unique variation, and it was common practice, if they were conquered or otherwise absorbed into a more powerful tribe, for their *gul* to be adopted, usually as a subsidiary element, into the victor's future compositions. *Gul* designs are found in many old and antique rugs from East Turkestan, Mongolia and Tibet, and also in contemporary items from the Chinese Sinkiang range and Tibetan/Nepalese/Indian rugs.

The ay-gul (pl. 9, and p. 10) is a variation of the usual Turkoman *gul* found in old East Turkestan and, to a lesser extent, Mongolian, Tibetan and some Chinese rugs. Its exact meaning is uncertain, but most authorities believe it to be a symbol of the moon. In contemporary rugs, it is found in the same range of items as other *guls*.

Medallion-and-corner designs (pls. 4, 6, 16) are the most frequently encountered compositions in *Chinese* and other oriental rugs. They consist of a central medallion, with echoing or contrasting motifs in the four corners, set against either an open or a decorated field. There are numerous variations on this theme, and the exact nature of the 'medallion-and-corner' is determined by the overall style of the range to which the rug belongs. For example, Persian-design rugs use the traditional *Persian/Islamic* 'book-cover' scheme (which is based on a worm's-eye view of the inside of a mosque dome, and derives its name from the patterned leather covers of the Koran). In contrast, rugs from the Standard Chinese and Antique Finish ranges may use this format with more traditional *Chinese* motifs – e.g. a coiled dragon as the central medallion with four smaller, uncoiled dragons in the corners.

Medallion-and-corner designs are found in all ranges of contemporary Chinese and Tibetan/Nepalese pile rugs, but are rarely, if ever, used in needlepoint and petit point, and only occasionally in kelims. This format is common to most groups of old and antique *Chinese* items, although it is especially associated with old Peking rugs and, to a lesser extent, those attributed to Kansu and Suiyuan, as well as East Turkestan, Tibetan and Mongolian rugs.

Aubusson and other Western designs have been widely used in Chinese rugs since the beginning of the 20th century, when North American and European importers began sending their own designs to be produced in China. The most influential of these were based on the opulent floral schemes pioneered, during the 17th and 18th centuries, by the Aubusson and Savonnerie workshops in France. Variations on these designs have been in constant use ever since, and today the Aubusson scheme is one of the most popular and distinctive designs in the Standard Chinese range (pl.21).

Since the late 1970s, there has been a dramatic acceleration in both the volume and diversity of Western, or Western-inspired, designs being adopted by both the Chinese and Tibetan/Nepalese rug-making industries. Some of these, particularly in China, are based on popular Western design movements (such as Art Nouveau, pl. 25), but the majority are the products of Western artists, who usually adapt traditional *Chinese* designs and motifs so that they conform to 'Western taste' (pls. 17, 18). Western designs are found primarily in the Standard Chinese, needlepoint, petit point and kelim ranges (pls. 19, 20), as well as in some Tibetan/Nepalese rugs. They are also used widely in tufted and hooked rugs (p. 28).

Floral designs employ a variety of leaf, frond and floral motifs in different overall formats. These schemes may employ an allover or repeating theme, or consist simply of floral or vegetal sprays set against an open or decorated field. Floral designs are also frequently used in conjunction with another standard format, especially medallion-and-corner schemes.

Allover and repeating floral formats are usually found in contemporary rugs belonging to the Sinkiang, Persian-design and, to a lesser extent, Antique Finish ranges, and also in some Tibetan/Nepalese rugs. In old and antique items, this format is closely associated with East Turkestan and Mongolian rugs, but is also found in items from other *Chinese* weaving groups. (See pls. 14, 19, 24.)

Three variations on the chrysanthemum

Simple floral formats are used extensively in contemporary needlepoint and petit point, and are also common in the Standard Chinese and, to a lesser extent, Antique Finish ranges, as well as being a popular scheme in Tibetan/Nepalese rugs. In old and antique items, simple floral formats are closely associated with Tibetan rugs, but can also be found in *Chinese* rugs from every region and group, although they are less common in items from Mongolia and East Turkestan. (See pls. 17, 18, 20.)

Floral designs used in conjunction with other formats (e.g. floral medallions) may be found in both contemporary and old items from every range and group (pls. 11, 21).

Mythological designs are based on figures, creatures and scenes from a broad array of religious, philosophical and legendary sources, and may be either naturalistic or more abstract and allusive in form. Natural-istic representations usually locate the focal figure or figures in a setting associated with either some aspect of their life (real or legendary), or which emphasizes the qualities they are believed to possess. For example, Buddha is usually shown sitting in the 'lotus' position with a *dorje* (p. 116) or other meditative symbol in his hand; Lao Tze is shown surrounded by his disciples, and Taoist immortals are frequently depicted carrying their individual talismen (e.g. flute, lotus pod). Where a person, creature or object has several aspects, the surroundings usually identify the specific aspect or quality represented.

Sometimes what appears to be a perfectly ordinary landscape or gathering of people will have strong religious, philosophical, legendary or mythological overtones. Some scenes depict characters re-enacting a legendary event (e.g. 'sages studying the symbol of *yin* and *yang*'; devotees making a 'pilgrimage to Shou Shan, the Hills of Longevity'; or 'the Yellow God, Hwang-Ti, ascending the throne'), which only those familiar with Chinese culture and history could hope to recognize. Others are even more obscure, and it is not uncommon for a simple landscape to possess a deep symbolic meaning, with hills representing dragons, trees and stones each symbolizing a specific 'soul substance' (p. 104), and the entire design dissected by invisible 'dragon veins'. (Dragon veins are invisible lines running from heaven to specific points on earth, which have a similar, although cosmic, function to the meridians on the human body used in acupuncture.)

In contemporary rugs, mythological designs are found primarily in items from the Tapestry range (pl. 41), and to a lesser degree in Standard Chinese and Antique Finish rugs. However, mythological elements may appear in items from almost any range of contemporary rugs, with the possible exceptions of Sinkiang and Persian-design. In old and antique items, mythological scenes are most closely associated with Paotao (pl. 42) and Ning-Hsia rugs, but are also frequently found in examples from other groups, although they are rare in East Turkestan and Mongolian rugs.

Animal designs are usually variations of mythological designs, because each animal has a specific symbolic significance, the exact meaning of which may be modified by its particular colour, form, and the context in which it is set. Sometimes the animal, bird or insect will be used in isolation (usually in an appropriate setting: birds on a branch, ducks in a pond), and sometimes they will be part of a larger interaction of flora, fauna and perhaps symbolic objects, patterns or iconographs (Chinese letters and glyphs, *shou* and *wan* forms).

Phoenix medallion

In the former, the meaning of the design is determined by the qualities associated with each animal, modified by variations in colour or detail. In the latter, the meaning is derived from a synthesis of the attributes associated with each motif, and often takes the form of a compound message (p. 115).

Animal designs are employed in numerous contemporary rugs from several ranges. They are often depicted naturalistically in tapestries (pl. 40) and, to a lesser extent, Standard Chinese and some Tibetan/Nepalese rugs. They are also used as elements in more complex compositions and landscapes. Animals are also found in many old and antique items, particularly those attributed to Paotao (where they are frequently naturalistic), Ning-Hsia, Suiyuan and Tibet (pls. 3, 38, 39, 42).

Dragon designs are a sub-group of both animal and mythological designs, but should be mentioned separately because of their importance to both Chinese beliefs and design, and also because there is a subtle distinction between rugs that employ dragons as part of their overall design, and authentic 'dragon-design' rugs. In the former, dragons appear in various shapes and sizes, as elements in a specific (often medallion-and-corner) format (pls. 15, 16). However, in 'authentic dragon rugs', the dragon is not only the major design element, but it also retains its mythological integrity, in that a specific aspect (e.g. bringer of thunder, guardian of the moon) is reinforced by its being reproduced in the appropriate colour and form, and surrounded by the traditional accessories. For example, when a dragon is shown in close proximity to a pearl, this stresses its role as guardian of the moon (the Pearl of Heaven), which it swallows to cause an eclipse and

A five-clawed imperial dragon with a flaming pearl

regurgitates to bring back the light. The meaning changes slightly when two dragons are shown fighting; according to legend, pearls fall to the ground when dragons fight, and, as pearls also symbolize 'a wish fulfilled', the 'message' of the design is one of good fortune and the wish that desires will come to fruition. Similarly, when dragons are seen with a 'flaming ball' (or pearl), it emphasizes their role as the lords of thunder, rain and lakes, because, according to legend, a dragon 'flames' when it comes into contact with water.

Dragon designs (pls. 2, 23) are found in the same ranges and groups of rugs as other animal designs, but feature especially strongly on old 'pillar' rugs (p. 31) and most contemporary items from Bhutan.

Tiger designs can be found, to a much lesser degree, across the same ranges and groups of *Chinese* rugs as dragon designs. However, when carpet dealers talk about 'Tiger rugs' they are normally referring to a style of rug associated with Tibet (p. 116, pls. 34–6).

The meaning of each design format is generally determined by the individual motifs, rather than the overall design. Consequently, a medallion-and-corner design employing dragons as its major decoration will have a different symbolic meaning from one that uses floral, bird or *shou* motifs. Similarly, the meaning of a floral scheme depends more on the specific flower, or flowers, used (e.g. chrysanthemums, pomegranates) than on whether it is reproduced in an allover, naturalistic or Tree-of-Life format. Exceptions to this rule are the Persian-design range, where *Persian/ Islamic* symbolism is retained, and Western designs – the Aubusson scheme, for example – in which the motifs are purely decorative and have no symbolic meaning whatsoever. Sinkiang rugs, both old and new, are a fusion between traditional *Chinese* and traditional *Persian/Islamic* symbolism (which places more emphasis on the meaning implicit in the format – e.g. prayer-rug, Tree-of-Life – than on the individual motifs); interpretations of designs used in these items should therefore take into account the fact that two different sets of cultural and symbolic values are at work.

Chinese symbolism

Chinese symbolism is drawn from a number of religious, philosophical, historical and legendary sources, the most influential of which are Buddhism, Taoism, Confucianism, and various myths, legends and magical beliefs, dating back to the animistic and shamanistic cults that are known to have been flourishing at the dawn of the Shang Dynasty (*c.* 1766 BC). Chinese symbolism differs from that of most other countries in two important respects: a) the belief that every object, animate or inanimate, has its own individual 'soul substance'; and b) that there is a mystical connection, or symbolic empathy, between an object and a quality that has a similar-sounding name.

Feng shui and other underlying principles
Feng shui (or *fung shui*) is the ancient Chinese science of geomancy, which is still widely practised in Chinese communities throughout the world. When Bruce Lee, the legendary film star and Kung Fu expert, died unexpectedly at the age of thirty-two, a Hong Kong newspaper immediately blamed it on bad *feng shui*, because shortly before his death a storm had blown down a tree overlooking his house, breaking the *bhat gwa* mirror (which traditionally deflects bad *feng shui*), leaving him exposed to evil influences.

According to the Chinese, almost every misfortune or disaster can be attributed to a person or place attracting bad *feng shui*. Similarly, good fortune and success are associated with the ability to attract good *feng shui*. Certain environments are believed to be intrinsically good or bad because of the specific relationship of the individual elements (both natural and man-made) to each other. Hills, for example, are *yang* and represent dragons; consequently, a house built on the side of a hill is likely to disturb the dragon (causing earthquakes or disasters), unless other environmental factors are modified to maintain a natural harmony. Such was the belief in *feng shui* during the imperial dynasties that temples, palaces and important buildings were, with few exceptions, built in accordance with *feng shui* principles. Even today, *feng shui* practitioners are often employed as consultants for new developments; and in Hong Kong, millions of dollars have been paid in compensation by the government to people claiming that their good *feng shui* has been damaged by official building programmes.

The allure of *feng shui* springs from its function as a physical manifestation of the natural laws and principles that the Chinese believe govern all of life. This belief transcends the particulars of Buddhism, Taoism and Confucianism, and sees nature as a living, breathing organism, made up of millions of independent but inextricably connected parts, each with its own individual material and spiritual quality. Consequently, the same laws that govern Chinese medicine, for example, can also be applied to art, nature and architecture, where a similar balance must be kept between the *yin* and *yang*, and other elemental forces, if health and harmony are to be maintained.

Modern *feng shui* is largely based on the work of Wang Chi and other Sung Dynasty scholars, who systematized the writings and recorded practices dating back to antiquity. The central tenet is that, in the beginning, there was one all-pervading abstract principle that caused the existence of all things. When it alternated between rest and movement – breathing in and breathing out – it produced the *yin* and the *yang*, the female and the male, that which yields and that which goes forth. The tension between these opposing forces caused the wind of life, the *ch'i*, to blow through the universe, providing the source of energy for all animate and inanimate things. The progress of the *ch'i* is governed by immutable laws (*li*) and mathematical principles (*so*), which are beyond the comprehension of ordinary mortals, but whose workings are discernible in nature and the outward form of the physical world (the *ying*).

The two main schools of *feng shui*, the Fukien and the Kiangsi, are based on an understanding of the four principles: *ch'i, li, so* and *ying*. The former school, also known as the Ancestral Hall, or Direction Method, lays particular emphasis on astrology and the hexagrams in the *I-Ching* (the Book of Changes, used to divine the underlying patterns of life). The latter, sometimes referred to as the School of Forms, concerns itself more with the formation of the landscape and its relationship with the *ch'i*, or cosmic breath.

Feng shui and design are inextricably connected because the 'spiritual/mystical' qualities associated with individual objects or creatures (trees, flowers etc.) are considered to be present to some degree in their pictorial representations. Consequently, it was not enough for a classical watercolour or ink landscape painting to be merely aesthetically harmonious; to bestow good fortune on the buyer, it also had to ensure that the mystical relationship between the hill, the tree, the water and the sky, for example, conformed to good *feng shui*. Similarly, certain animals, plants and objects were favourably associated with each other, and an artist was inviting misfortune if he placed incompatible creatures or objects together. These basic principles of composition are evident in numerous rug designs, and, despite the growing commercialization of rug production, can still be found in many items coming onto the market today.

Soul substance, according to Chinese belief, is present in everything, whether human, animal, bird, vegetable or mineral. The difference in 'soul substance' between certain animals and plants, especially those belonging to the same *genus*, may be extremely subtle, but it is nevertheless unique to each individual species of flower, for example, rather than to flowers as a whole; the soul substance of a chrysanthemum is not the same as that of a peony or lotus flower, and the soul substance of a tiger is radically different from that of an elephant or horse.

The potency of the soul substance in individual plants, animals or precious stones etc., varies considerably – from the ability to cure a minor illness to the capacity for prolonging life – and everything is carefully graded according to both its specific properties and its overall strength.

The Chinese also believe that soul substance can be transmitted by contact or association. In its simplest manifestation, this is the basis of Chinese herbalism; certain plants possess certain properties, or qualities, and by drinking or eating them a person will draw those properties into him or herself. For example, if a person's *yin* is depleted, the patient will be given herbs and foods that are rich in *yin*. Similarly, growing chrysanthemums in your garden will help to promote longevity; mandarin ducks on your pond will ensure the fidelity of your spouse, and meditating on a tiger skin will help you attain the tiger's virility and strength. Nor is this 'mystical osmosis' confined to association with the actual creature or object; an image is also believed to contain a degree of its subject's soul substance, so placing yourself in close proximity to a painting, sculpture or rug will have a similar effect.

The ling are spiritual beings who inhabit every aspect of the natural and mythological world. There are an almost infinite number, all with their own powers, characteristics and natural affinities with specific objects, creatures (both real and mythological), plants and natural elements (e.g. east wind, west wind, well-water, sea, streams). They are, in many ways, an animate extension of soul substance, but because they are quasi-human in character, they can be mischievous and unpredictable, unless guarded against or appeased. As with soul substance, different objects and living entities attract different qualities of *ling*; the more potent the host, the more powerful are the *ling* it will attract. Consequently, in the hierarchy of *ling*-bearing creatures the dragon houses the strongest and highest number, followed by the phoenix, unicorn and tortoise.

Chinese alchemy has a subtle but extremely potent influence on Chinese designs, and although there are few overtly 'alchemical' symbols employed, its central tenet – the search for immortality – is an ever-present theme (p. 54). In contrast to most Western societies the Chinese still largely venerate age, so the symbolic purpose of most Chinese motifs is to promote long life. Many motifs also have more specific meanings or associations, but the promotion of long life is the constant factor (e.g. *shou* – good luck and long life; deer – career success and long life).

Shared meanings The Chinese believe that all things are connected, and therefore that objects which are similar in one respect (e.g. colour or shape) must also share other characteristics. Similarly, because of their belief that the soul substances of things in close proximity tend to rub off on one another, they perceive a symbolic connection between an object and its use or association. Consequently, deer, which were hunted by the rich, have come to symbolize wealth and authority; and peonies, traditionally cultivated in the gardens of the nobility, have evolved an association with rank, material comfort and well-being.

Homonyms are words that sound the same but have different meanings. The Chinese believe that this is not coincidental, and that if an object (bat) and a concept (happiness) share the same pronunciation, the object takes on the quality of the concept. For example, as the characters for 'stag' and 'emolument' (profit from employment) are pronounced in exactly the same way, stags symbolize career success. Homonyms are found in most languages, but outside China they rarely indicate an underlying symbolic connection between the objects and concepts concerned.

A mixture of motifs is common in most *Chinese* designs, and does not necessarily indicate a complex symbolic message. Frequently, the motifs have no physical or metaphorical connection with each other; they are merely isolated elements in the overall design, and should be interpreted as such. For example, in a floral design rug with *shou* or fret (p. 112) motifs in the border, the major symbolic intent of the design is normally determined by the type of flower employed, while the border motifs are of minor symbolic importance, and should be interpreted simply as additional tokens of good luck and long life.

However, if the main design is composed of two or more motifs that are either physically connected or thematically integral to the overall design, then it is usually safe to assume that a complex message or philosophical statement is being expressed. For example, a repeating 'bat and *shou*' allover scheme can be roughly translated as 'good luck (*shou*) and happiness (bat)'. If the same design employed peach and peony motifs, however, the interpretation would be 'may you live long (peach) and prosper (peony)'. It is important to remember that most Chinese motifs have more than one meaning, and when two or three are used in conjunction, there may be several possible, perhaps equally valid, interpretations.

Medallions and mandalas differ in terms of their symbolic intent, rather than form. Almost any large central motif may be referred to as a medallion, regardless of its symbolic significance, but the term is perhaps best used to describe motifs that are either drawn directly from *Persian/*

Islamic designs (e.g. medallion-and-corner), or other non-Chinese decorative schemes (Aubusson).

A mandala is arguably the most potent and universal symbol of Buddhism, Hinduism and, to a lesser extent, Taoist thought; it acts as a visual metaphor for the Universe, Creation, the Wheel of Life and Eternity, and is used as the focus for meditation. In common with the Christian cross, it can be reproduced in several ways, each having a slightly different spiritual variation. The inner decoration (e.g. bats, clouds, *shou* motifs) serves as a more specific meditative focal point, channelling the particular qualities or areas of understanding that need to be explored: for example, the harmony of energies implicit in the *yin* and *yang*, or the need to remain pure in a corrupt environment, as symbolized by the lotus.

In contemporary rugs, it is generally safe to assume that Persian-design and most Sinkiang (East Turkestan) items will employ medallions rather than mandalas; the same is true of rugs that use Western, or Western-inspired, designs.

The meaning of individual motifs

Chinese motifs can be divided into several distinct categories, either by type (plant, animal etc.) or by origin (Buddhist, Taoist, mythological). However, such is the complex and multi-faceted nature of even the most common symbols that such divisions are always somewhat arbitrary. The dragon, for example, is common to both Buddhism and Taoism, manifesting slightly different aspects of its 'symbolic' nature in each, as well as appearing in numerous folk tales and legends. It also appears frequently in its more abstract, metaphorical guises, either as hills or invisible 'dragon veins' (p. 101) within an apparently naturalistic landscape.

It is important, therefore, to remember that the following categories are not hard and fast divisions, and one should always be conscious of the different, and sometimes contradictory, influences from which the symbolic meanings of most motifs are drawn.

Animals and mythological beasts

Dragons are arguably the single most important mythological symbol in *Chinese* culture and art, and the one most frequently used in carpet design (p. 24). There is no doubt that the Chinese dragon is unique to China and the countries within its sphere of influence, but there are numerous similarities with the dragon lore of other cultures, from South America to Celtic Britain and Ancient Egypt. Essentially, the dragon is a hybrid, a fusion of the snake-god and the bird-god (the *nagas* and *garudas* of Hindu/Buddhist mythology), adapted to local environments and spiritual beliefs. In maritime cultures, for example, it frequently takes the form of a fish. According to Celtic and Icelandic legends, the salmon was believed to be a manifestation of a dragon; when the Norse god Loki took on the form of a salmon, he caused earthquakes when he turned, and Finn (or Fionn) of Gaelic legend ate the 'Salmon of Knowledge' to become a seer. An ancient Chinese poem ends with the lines: 'If we do not seek the dragons, they also will not seek us', a sentiment also expressed in a traditional Gaelic (Scottish) poem to Bride (later Christianized to St Bridget); 'I will not molest the serpent, and the serpent will not molest me.'

Ancient Chinese texts describe the evolution of the dragon thus: 'A water snake changes after five hundred years into a *kiao* (a serpent-dragon), after a thousand years a *kiao* becomes a *kiao-lung* (a dragon with fish scales), five hundred years later it changes into a *kioh-lung* (a horned dragon), and after a further thousand years it evolves into a *ying-lung* (a winged-dragon)'. This, and similar accounts, of the dragon's evolution illustrate the way in which the concept of the dragon developed over the centuries, picking up various attributes and qualities along the way.

The Chinese dragon can take on any form or disguise – from a white stag to a young girl – and also change its essential 'dragon shape' and colour, according to the specific qualities or aspects that are being expressed. However, there are certain consistent physical attributes. An ancient text informs us that a dragon has 'the head of a camel, the horns of a stag, the eyes of a demon, the ears of a cow, the neck of a snake, the belly of a clam, the scales of a carp, the claws of an eagle, and the soles of a tiger.' It also has a lump on its head, a *ch'ih muh*, which it uses like an inflatable gas-bag to hover in the air. Its body is made up of three jointed parts: the head and shoulders, the shoulders and breast, and the breast and tail. It is covered with 117 scales, 81 of which radiate *yang* and good influence, and 36 *yin* and bad influence; under its throat the number of scales is reversed. The male, distinguished from the female by its whiskers, stubbier nose and undulating horn, is usually portrayed with a luminous pearl under its chin. A horned (male) dragon is called a *k'iu-lung*, and a hornless (female) a *ch'i-lung*.

Dragons in carpet designs may be either male or female, winged or wingless, and manifest any of their numerous aspects. They are most frequently portrayed coiled,

fighting or playing with a flaming ball or pearl (p. 102). Dragons have been closely associated with the emperor and imperial power for most of China's recorded history; this connection was brought to the forefront of rug-making during the Ch'ing Dynasty, when an imperial decree established that 'five-clawed' dragons (pl. 2) could only appear on rugs destined for the emperor and for first and second rank princes, 'four-clawed' dragons, on items for lower-ranked princes, and scaleless 'bird-and-serpent' (or primitive) dragons on those for fifth-rank princes and certain other high officials. Three-clawed, or water dragons, were not as closely associated with the emperor, and rarely appear on old and antique rugs. (The number of claws in rugs made after 1912, when China became a republic, has no link whatsoever with imperial usage.) This association with imperial power has tended to overshadow all the other symbolic aspects of the dragon, and they are generally associated with the desired imperial attributes of power, authority, strength, wisdom, divine protection and, of course, long life.

The phoenix, like the dragon, is a composite of the physical and *ling* (spiritual) aspects of a number of creatures, and can be traced back to the Shang Dynasty, when it was used as a clan, or 'totem', emblem. It is said to have the forehead of a crane, the crown of a mandarin drake, the throat of a swallow, the bill of a fowl, the neck of a snake, the tail of a fish, the back of a tortoise and the scales of a dragon. Alternatively, it has been described as a combination of a crane, a pheasant, a peacock and a serpent. The phoenix appears in the mythology of countries throughout the world as a symbol of rebirth, and is often associated, along with other birds, with transporting souls to the Afterworld. Like the dragon, it seems to have its origin in the fusion between the old serpent and bird gods, but whereas the dragon's evolution appears to have followed that of the serpent (or *naga*), the phoenix has stayed closer to the bird (or *garuda*).

The Chinese phoenix is often portrayed as the female version of the dragon, although both creatures have male and female manifestations. (The male phoenix is referred to as the *feng* and the female as the *huang*; both sexes are included in the term *fenghuang*.) It came to be linked closely with the empress and the associated qualities of grace, beauty, elegance, nobility and refinement. It later developed into a symbol of good fortune and good government – no doubt with a little imperial encouragement of the belief that one could look for no better fortune than to live under a wise and benign ruler – and is generally used today as a symbol of happiness, good fortune, peace, beauty and refinement. The five traditional colours of the phoenix – red, violet, blue, yellow and black – are often associated with the five Confucian virtues (see p. 53).

In carpet designs the phoenix (pl. 31) may appear in isolation, or in the company of a dragon (when it usually represents the female counter to the dragon's maleness, harmonizing the *yin* and *yang*), or as part of a specific mythological scene – for example, the *Danfeng* ('the vermilion phoenix facing the sun') or the *Bai niao chao feng* ('phoenix holding an audience for a thousand birds').

Tigers are the traditional *Chinese* 'were' animal and enemy of the dragon, and are associated with strength, virility and the west. Lords of the mountains and woods, they are joint controllers (with dragons) of the winds and water, and embodiments of the god of war, as well as being the chief protectors of graves and the souls of the dead. Tiger symbolism, in conjunction with that of the dragon, is an integral part of *feng shui*. (See also p. 116.)

Lions (pl. 38) are symbols of valour and energy, and are also one of the traditional guardians of Buddha and Buddhism. Their role as 'protector' was later absorbed into general Chinese mythology, and for centuries stone or bronze lions have been used, in their capacity as 'defenders of law' and 'protectors of important and sacred buildings' (p. 52), at the entrances to courts, temples and government and commercial institutions – the male on the east, usually holding an engraved ball in its right paw,

Chinese lion playing with a ball

and the female on the west, caressing a cub with her left paw.

Fo dogs (or lion-dogs) symbolize strength and courage, and, like lions, which they closely resemble, were companions of Buddha and the guardians of Buddhist holy places. They appear frequently in old and antique rugs (pls. 3, 38), and are believed to be based on either pekinese or chows, or perhaps a combination of both.

Horses are closely connected with both the nobility and the military, and white horses in particular were associated with carrying Buddhist teaching into India. Consequently, they symbolize wealth, prestige, mobility and the spreading of knowledge. A horse tethered to a tree is a favourite subject in many old and antique rugs.

Unicorns are found in Chinese mythology in two forms (one with the body of a stag, the other with the body of an ox) and are supposed to appear when sages are born. They are associated with wisdom and the power of healing.

Stags, as distinct from stag-unicorns, symbolize emolument (p. 105), and are also

The image of a horse tethered to a tree
is typical of old Suiyuan rugs

associated with longevity, due to their
reputed ability to find the *ling-chi*, or sacred
fungus of immortality (p. 112).

Monkeys sometimes feature in Chinese carpets, usually as representations of the
monkey-god during one of his numerous
adventures (pl. 42).

Tortoises rarely appear in Chinese carpets
and designs, despite being one of the most
potent symbols of longevity, because one
of their most common dialect names,
wamba, is a rather vulgar invective.

Toads are the familiars (mystical companions) of Lui-hai, the patron of monetary
transactions, and are therefore symbols of
good luck in business dealings. They are
rarely found in rug designs.

Bats (pl. 6) are extremely popular motifs
in Chinese rug designs, and symbolize
happiness, because the Chinese characters
for 'bat' and 'happiness' (*fu*) sound the same
when spoken aloud (p. 105). Bats often
appear in conjunction with other motifs (pp.
115, 119, 127).

The five noxious animals – snakes, lizards,
scorpions, frogs and centipedes – are those
whose *ling* turn into mischievous spirits
when old, and are consequently rarely used
in rug designs. The scorpion, however, is
a common motif in East Turkestan rugs.

Birds, butterflies and fish
Cranes (pl. 40) are the traditional companions and messengers of Taoist immortals, and have therefore come to symbolize
long life and the knowledge of immortality.
They also became the emblem of high
government office during the Manchu Dynasty, and thus have associations with rank
and status. (See p. 56).

Storks, especially if blue, were companions
of the Queen of the Immortals, and hence
symbolize longevity.

Geese have no clear mythological or phonetic links with specific qualities, but are
generally seen as symbolic of longevity,
freedom and independence. A single wild
goose often symbolizes the joy of solitude.

Magpies are associated with good luck –
the Chinese word for magpie means 'bird
of joy' – and magpies nesting near your
home indicate a positive change in fortune.
They are also believed to be 'good omen
birds': magpies chattering outside your
house signify the arrival of welcome guests,
and hearing the bird's cry while devising
a scheme is a sign that it will succeed.

Five bats surrounding a *shou* medallion:
wufu pengshou

Medallion with mandarin ducks: lifelong fidelity and affection

Carp medallion – symbolic of achievement, success and long life

Mandarin ducks are symbolic of conjugal fidelity and affection, and are normally represented in pairs (male and female).

Paradise flycatchers, or ribbon birds, symbolize long life because of the homophonic links between the bird's name (*shou-dai-niao*) and the character for longevity (*shou*).

Chinese bulbuls represent conjugal fidelity; and when shown in pairs, as they usually are, this extends to living in conjugal bliss through to a ripe old age.

Butterflies (pl. 5) are common motifs in Chinese design, and are generally taken as symbolizing happiness and good luck, because of the phonetic similarity between the words for butterfly (*hu*) and happiness (*fu*), which are almost indistinguishable in many Chinese dialects.

Four variations on the butterfly motif

Fish have a number of different symbolic meanings to the Chinese. There is a homophonic connection between the word for fish (*yu*) and the word for excess or superfluity; which is usually extended to mean 'abundance' or 'abundant wealth'. A pair of fishes is a common betrothal gift, signifying a happy and fruitful marriage, and is also one of the 'eight Buddhist symbols' for averting evil (pp. 55 and 114). In mythology, they are also frequently referred to as the carriers of souls. Certain species of fish have specific symbolic meanings, but, with the exception of carp, few individual species are ever represented in carpet designs.

Carp are the most symbolically important and widely used fish species in Chinese designs. They have a number of different meanings, especially the homophonic link with the word for profit, or benefit, and association with the carp's real, or legendary, capacity for perseverance, which it shares with dragons. (Fish that swam through the 'Dragon's Gate' rapids, at Longmen, were believed to turn into dragons. Carp also possess some of the dragon's physical characteristics – whiskers and scales.) Carp therefore symbolize the ability to overcome adversity and achieve eminence and success. They are also symbolic of longevity, because it is believed they can live for ever, and will only die if they are killed by outside forces or lose the will to grow.

Flowers and plants

Peonies (pls. 5, 28, 29, 32) are the national flower of Tibet and the northern Chinese province of Honan (Henan), and are generally regarded as the 'King of Flowers'. The Chinese name for peony, *mudan*, literally means 'vermilion man'. It was traditionally cultivated in the gardens of noble families and has therefore come to symbolize wealth, nobility, beauty and refined affection. Peonies also symbolize spring, and are one of the most common flowers in *Chinese* designs.

Lotus flowers are closely associated with Buddhism, because the Buddhist paradise is strewn with lotus blossoms, and Buddha is often depicted sitting on the Sumera Seat, or Lotus Throne. They symbolize purity and perfection, probably because, despite growing in swamps and marshes, the lotus retains its purity, untainted by its surroundings, in the same way that people who are morally pure will be unaffected by the evil and corruption around them. The lotus has two names in Chinese; one is a homonym of the word for 'peace and harmony', and the other means repeated good fortune. The lotus symbolizes summer, and its seed pod represents fertility and progeny.

Chrysanthemums (p. 101) symbolize autumn and a peaceful old age (wine containing dried chrysanthemum petals is believed to aid longevity) and are one of the most popular floral motifs in *Chinese* designs.

Plum blossoms are a general symbol of longevity because of the great age to which plum trees have been known to survive. In rug designs, flowers with five petals normally represent the plum, and denote the 'five blessings' of long life, wealth, peace and health, love of virtue, and a natural death. Plum blossom also symbolizes winter.

Daffodils represent good luck, and are an alternative symbol of winter.

Peaches are the traditional 'food of the gods' in Chinese mythology, and are therefore symbolic of longevity and the quest for immortality. They are one of the principal ingredients in the elixir of life, sought by Taoist alchemists, and objects made from any part of the tree or fruit were used to combat evil spirits. Peaches are also associated with young brides and spring – the customary time for weddings.

The Buddha's hand citron (fo-shou) gets its name because it resembles a human hand, and is symbolic of wealth, honour and serenity.

Pomegranates, which symbolize fertility, due to the numerous seeds contained in the fruit, were used as design motifs in Central Asia before being brought into China some time before the last century BC. The pomegranate is a common motif on old East Turkestan and contemporary Sinkiang rugs, particularly as part of a Tree-of-Life scheme (pl. 10).

Modern border combining naturalistic peony and fret motifs

The fungus of immortality (ling-chi) is a species of fungus which, according to legend, could only be found by the phoenix or stag. It supposedly grows in remote mountain regions and on the 'Three Islands of the Immortals' of Taoist legend, and is a potent symbol of longevity. In rug designs, it is usually seen in conjunction with other longevity motifs.

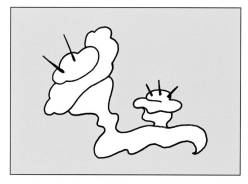

The *ling-chi*, or fungus of immortality

Bamboo (below) is one of the most common motifs in Chinese art, and its physical qualities – strength, flexibility and endurance – are symbolic of the same human virtues, particularly on the mental, emotional and spiritual planes. Bamboo is also connected with 'auspicious good luck', because the Chinese name for bamboo (*zhu*) is a homonym of the word for wish. (See p. 48.)

Trees in carpet designs are normally depicted either as extensions of their own fruit or blossoms, or in conjunction with another, usually animal or bird, motif. In the former, their meaning can be assumed to be that of their fruit (plum, peach etc.); in the latter, they are generally symbols of longevity.

Characters, patterns and objects

Shou characters (pls. 5, 15, 26) are symbols of longevity, and linked to both the Taoist quest for immortality and the Confucian belief in the wisdom of old age. There are numerous variations – giving someone a hundred different *shou* characters written on a piece of paper, representing the wish that they might live to be a hundred, was a popular custom in ancient China. In carpet designs they are usually stylized versions of the circular and elongated forms.

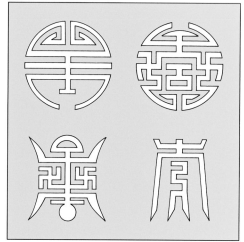

Shou, fu and *xi* characters

Fu and xi characters operate on exactly the same principle as *shou* characters, but are based on the word for happiness, rather than long life.

Other Chinese characters may occasionally be employed in rug designs. However, all Chinese characters used in this way are generally referred to as *shou*, or *fu*, designs.

Fret designs is the collective term for a variety of lineal, interlocking motifs resembling a maze viewed from above, and employed primarily as border designs (e.g. above, p. 99, and pls. 4, 6, 13).

The Lei wen (or Thunder pattern) first appeared on prehistoric pottery, and is believed to signify happiness and long life. A jagged line, resembling the letter 'Z', is a common symbol for forked lightning in several cultures, and the 'Thunder pattern' (or 'Thunder scroll') is not unlike a series of similar interlocking forms. *Lei wen* is the Chinese name for the swastika, but in rug designs the term is normally reserved for this more specific scrolling pattern (above).
Wan motifs (pl. 6) are variations on the basic fret design, and are believed to be complex, interlocking versions of the swastika motif. *Wan* is the Chinese character for ten thousand, and so this design represents ten thousand happinesses.

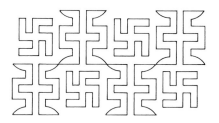

The swastika has been ascribed several meanings – including happiness, the heart of Buddha and the number ten thousand – and derives its name from two ancient Sanskrit words meaning 'well-being', or 'good fortune'. We know that it was an emblem for the supreme god among early Aryan civilizations, and that it was later adopted as a symbol of the Buddha by the Jains (a religious sect that arose out of Hinduism and Buddhism), who introduced it into China around 200 BC. The Empress Wu (*c.* AD 684–704) ordered that it should be used as a sign for the sun, as it had been in India several centuries before, and in Buddhist symbolism it became connected with *karma*, or the cycle of life. The true swastika has its short arms facing to the right, signifying an anti-clockwise rotation, which follows the daily motion of the sun from east to west. (See pl. 9).

The sauvastika is a mirror image of the swastika (i.e. the short arms face to the left), and, in Hinduism, it was believed that the swastika and the sauvastika represented aspects of the male and female principles, as manifest in the god Ganesh (lord of knowledge and learning) and the goddess Kali (devourer of the souls of the dead and guardian of 'dark', or 'forbidden' knowledge). Both the swastika and sauvastika are common symbols in *Chinese* rug designs.
The Ju'i sceptre is used by the highest deity in heaven and symbolizes a wish, or the hope that a wish be fulfilled. It is usually represented on rugs as a cloud with a short tail (pl. 2).
Vases (p'ing) are common motifs in *Chinese* designs and generally symbolize peace.
Tables (an) signify tranquility, and in carpet designs are usually found in conjunction with other motifs – e.g., a vase on a table, symbolizing peace and tranquility.

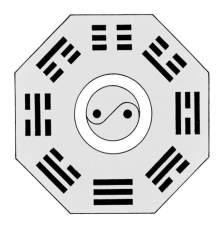

Yin/yang wheels (above) symbolize the harmony between the female (*yin*) and male (*yang*) principles. The symbol's origins predate the major Chinese religious and philosophical systems, but it has subsequently been absorbed into each. (See pl. 1.)
The eight tetragrams (pa kua) represent the eight natural elements – heaven, wind, earth, fire, water, mountain, thunder and cloud – and symbolize the harmony and cardinal points of nature. They are often used in conjunction with the *yin/yang* wheel (above).

Ji (or tridents) have a homophonic connection with the words for 'good omen' and 'grade', or 'job status'.

Coins, as one would expect, symbolize prosperity. However, old Chinese coins normally had a hole in the centre so they could be carried on a piece of string, and these are also used as symbols for the 'eye', or something made visible to the eye.

Bogu objects (or 'The grand collection of antiques') are a combination of various bronze, jade and porcelain objects, often represented on a foliate background, that were considered to be the greatest artistic treasures of the Sung Dynasty (the era from which the design originated). There is no universally accepted symbolic meaning behind these objects, but they are believed to signify beauty, harmony, refinement and the pinnacle of artistic achievement.

Religious and philosophical symbols

Most *Chinese* symbols could legitimately be placed in this category, but there are certain motifs, or groups of motifs, that have specific connections with a particular religious or philosophical movement when reproduced together, or in a particular context, in rug designs.

The eight Taoist symbols (p. 53) are objects carried by, or associated with, the eight Taoist immortals (*pa hsien*), and are used in designs to represent the presence, teaching and attributes of each individual immortal. As with everything in Taoism, the symbolic meaning of each motif is complex and multi-layered. However, the following attributions are generally accepted: 1) *sword*: supernatural power; 2) *staff and gourd*: alchemic transmutation and the concoction of medicines; 3) *lotus pod*: omnipotence, the seat or centre of power; 4) *flute*: the power to conjure magic; 5) *bamboo*: the ability to tell fortunes and divine the future; 6) *fan*: the power to revive the souls of the dead; 7) *castanets*: the power to soothe and banish evil influences; 8) *basket of flowers*: knowledge of the 'soul substances' of plants and flowers. (See pls. 1, 2.)

The eight Buddhist symbols (p. 55) are associated with the mysterious shapes that, according to legend, appeared in Buddha's footprints on his visit to Kusinagara in *c.* 487 BC. The objects represented by these shapes are believed to have the power to banish evil, and relate to the spiritual qualities and truths that the believer should try to develop. 1) *Canopy*: protection afforded to the weak by the strong (on a mundane level, it relates to official rank); 2) *lotus flower*: purity; 3) *umbrella*: personal dignity and authority (on a mundane level, it relates to the protection of the state); 4) *vase containing heavenly elixir*: enduring peace and a symbol of the need to be a receptacle of virtue and good achievements; 5) *conch shell*: calling to prayer and meditation; 6) *fishes*: abundance and marital harmony, both on a personal and cosmic level; 7) *wheel*: the cycle of life, destiny, *karma* (also the majesty of the law, both mundane and cosmic); 8) *endless knot* (pl. 8): eternity, destiny; the cycle of life and mysterious connection of all things – physical and spiritual, material and non-material, human and divine. (See pls. 1, 3.)

The eight precious things, from the Book of Rites

The eight precious things are taken from the 'One Hundred Symbols' in the 'Book of Rites', and represent a fusion of Taoist, Buddhist and Confucian beliefs, which form what might be described as 'collective' Chinese philosophy. 1) *pearl*: purity and perfection; 2) *coin*: wealth; 3) *books*: the value of learning; 4) *empty rhombus*: victory and collective prosperity; 5) *full rhombus*: painting and the wealth derived from art; 6) *musical stone*: blessing; 7) *rhinoceros-horn*: resistance to poison, both physical and spiritual; 8) *artemisia leaf*: dignity and protection. (The origin of this last meaning is attributed to a rebel leader, during the T'ang Dynasty, who was so moved by the courage and dignity shown by a mother protecting her children that he nailed a bunch of artemisia leaves to her door as a sign that her home should not be entered.)

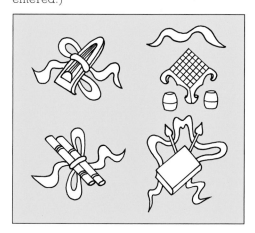

The four gentlemanly accomplishments

The four gentlemanly accomplishments (pl. 1) are based on the Confucian qualities deemed necessary for a man of nobility and learning. 1) *Lute*: proficiency at music; 2) *chessboard*: skill at chess and other games; 3) *scrolls*: the ability to paint and draw; 4) *books*: mastery of language and poetry.

Landscape motifs

When used in isolation, or outside the context of a naturalistic scene, they usually have the following symbolic meanings.

Clouds may be found either as 'floating clouds' on the field (below), or as 'cloud-band patterns' employed mainly in borders (pl. 7). Their meaning is unclear, but they are believed to be variations of the *ju'i* sceptre (when floating) and of the *Lei wen* (when cloudband), signifying wish-fulfilment and long life. (See pls. 26, 38.)

Mountains and sea are usually found together, and symbolize long life (mountains) and good fortune (sea, p. 43). In a stylized form, they are frequently employed as border designs (e.g. pls. 32, 33, 38).

Compound motifs

It is common practice in *Chinese* designs to combine two, or more, individual motifs to create a (compound) symbolic message (pl. 5). For example, a vase (peace) on a table (tranquility), off-set by a *ju'i* sceptre, could be interpreted as 'May you find peace and tranquility according to your wishes'. However, there are certain standard 'compound motifs', which, because of their popularity and the traditional, unambiguous nature of their message, should be viewed as specific motifs in their own right.

Bat and coins Immediate happiness, or happiness arising before your eyes.

Five bats encircling a rounded shou (p. 109), known as the *wufu pengshou* (literally, 'five bats lift-up longevity'), is generally taken as bestowing the 'five blessings' (p. 111).

Bat and three peaces signify the hope for sustained happiness throughout a long life.

Peach, pomegranate and Buddha's hand citron express the hope for prosperity and official honour, leading to abundant happiness throughout a long life.

Pine, plum and bamboo trees, known as the three friends (*suihan sanyou*), are symbolic of friendship and the ability to withstand adversity through the help of noble friends.

Plum, bamboo, chrysanthemum and orchid are known as the *si junzi*, or the 'four men of noble character', and seem to be connected to the development of Confucian virtues.

Crane, stag and toon tree, often referred to as the *helu tongchun*, symbolizes the wish for official promotion in springtime. It was a popular design on old Chinese (particularly Paotao) rugs.

Crane standing in the rising tide signifies the hope for promotion to the first degree in the imperial court.

Fungus (ling chi) in a vase on a table is usually interpreted as 'may your wish for peace and security be granted'.

Three ji (tridents) in a vase (below) express the hope of being promoted by three official degrees.

Egret, lotus and 'withered' lotus leaf signify the desire for success in passing official examinations.

Tibetan designs

Tibetan rug designs are very similar to those found in Chinese rugs, and, with slight variations, much of the religious and mythological symbolism, both in appearance and meaning, is the same. There are, of course, some differences: Tibet does not use homonymic associations or share the Chinese obsession with longevity and the desire to attract 'good fortune'. Although religious motifs are used in Tibetan rugs, there is a general reluctance to employ the most sacred Buddhist symbols in anything as worldly as a rug. In addition, there are some very distinct designs that are unique to traditional Tibetan weaving; although contemporary Chinese copies of these schemes are made.

Tiger rugs (pls. 34–6) are based on tiger pelts, rather than live animals. The design may be quite realistic or highly abstracted, but it always reproduces the tiger as a flat, two-dimensional form. Symbolically, tigers have several meanings (p. 108), but Tiger rugs are frequently associated with Tantric meditation, and it is believed that they may have been used as a substitute for real tiger pelts during advanced Tantric yoga practices.

Some Tibetan rugs contain more naturalistic representations of living tigers, but these are not necessarily classed as Tiger rugs, and their symbolic meaning may be more akin to the other aspects of tiger lore. Copies and modern variations of old Tiger rugs are now produced in contemporary items from the Tibetan/Nepalese ranges.

Snow leopards (pl. 39), the national animal of Tibet, are featured, often in pairs, on numerous old and contemporary rugs; they are generally held to symbolize strength, dignity and independence.

The chessboard design (pl. 27) is found on a number of contemporary rugs, from Romania to China, but seems to have originated in Tibet; its symbolism is obscure, and interpretations range from its being simply a copy of a patchwork quilt or chessboard, to symbolizing the constant juxtaposition of *yin* and *yang*, light and dark, day and night.

A dorje is a small cruciform object used in meditation, and is often seen in portraits of the Buddha, who will frequently have a *dorje* in one hand and a bell in the other. In Tibet, *Dorje dollock* is an important spiritual being, and variations of the *dorje* are common in both old and contemporary Tibetan rugs.

Chapter VI

Old and antique rugs

No one is certain exactly when, or by whom, the first *Chinese* rugs were made. There are a handful of rugs still in existence which have been attributed to the latter part of the Ming Dynasty (1368–1644), but the vast majority of surviving 'old' rugs were made no earlier than the 19th and, possibly, 18th centuries. However, we know that rugs were in use throughout China during the T'ang Dynasty (618–907), and perhaps earlier, because of references to rugs and carpets in official documents, letters, paintings and poems.

Whether these rugs were actually made in China, or imported from Persia (Iran), or one of the surrounding nomadic cultures, is open to debate. The techniques of pile rug weaving in the Far East almost certainly originated in East Turkestan, or possibly Mongolia, and were later imported into China proper, either directly or indirectly. However it is impossible to pinpoint exactly when this took place, or when the ethnic (Han) Chinese started weaving rugs themselves. (See Chapter IV for a history of rug-making in China and Chapter VII for a discussion of rug-making in the 20th century.)

Chinese weaving groups

China proper, as opposed to the wider *Chinese* sphere of influence, is generally defined as the area inside the Great Wall, plus the four provinces of Inner Mongolia (Suiyuan, Ning-Hsia, Chahar and Jehol) that border its northern frontier; it is the items from this area that dealers refer to as authentic Chinese rugs.

It is impossible, because of the absence of firm historical evidence, to include useful information on all the individual weaving centres that have existed in China. We know that several operated at different periods in a variety of locations, particularly in the colder northern districts; but, with a few exceptions, we know almost nothing about the type of rugs they produced.

There are a few centres, however, about which we do have information, and these are generally accepted as constituting the traditional Chinese weaving groups. It is by no means certain that all the characteristics attributed to rugs from these groups are founded in historical fact; and, although it is generally true that each centre produced the type of rugs with which it is now associated, similar rugs may well have been produced elsewhere. The following weaving groups are therefore synonymous with a particular style and quality of rug, rather than the only place where such items were made. Rugs that cannot be attributed to one of these groups are normally marketed simply as 'Chinese', although in practice dealers will often try to place an unattributed item in a specific group.

Peking and the nearby port of Tientsin are referred to as having workshops as far back as the Yuan Dynasty (*c.* 1279–1368). However, 'Peking rugs', as understood by dealers and collectors, are items with certain unifying characteristics, dating from the Ch'ing Dynasty (*c.* 1644–1911), which may or may not have been made in Peking. They are generally of medium to good quality, and often feature *shou* or other 'symbolic' medallions, as well as a variety of Buddhist, Taoist, Confucian and floral motifs, usually on an open field. Various colour schemes may be employed, although blues and creams are common. (See pls. 5, 11.)

Variations on other classic 'Peking designs' are also used in contemporary rugs, especially in the Standard Chinese and Antique Finish ranges (pls. 12–14).

Towards the end of the 19th and beginning of the 20th centuries, the workshops in Peking and Tientsin became closely associated (at least in the West) with the more Western-inspired designs produced to satisfy American and European tastes; contemporary rugs with Aubusson or other Western-inspired designs are often referred to as 'Pekings'. (See pls. 17, 18, 21, 22.)

Suiyuan, one of the border provinces of Inner Mongolia, is generally accepted, in terms of rug-making, as part of China proper. Rugs have been woven in the region for centuries, but, for dealers and collectors, Suiyuan rugs date from the Ch'ing Dynasty, and possess specific characteristics – although similar items may have been made earlier. Suiyuan rugs are arguably the easiest of all old Chinese rugs to recognize because they are generally fairly small, with a thicker than average pile, and frequently consist of designs produced exclusively in various shades of blue. Their favourite schemes are fret-medallions (pl. 6), stylized peonies, swastikas and other geometric emblems, and a horse or deer tethered beneath a tree (p. 109).

In contemporary rugs, traditional Suiyuan designs are reproduced primarily in the Antique Finish range.

Kansu is a northern frontier province, slightly west of Suiyuan, on the Chinese side of the Great Wall, which produces rugs that are very similar to those made in Suiyuan. Kansu rugs use the same repertoire of designs, and possess the same overall character and 'feel' as Suiyuans, but tend to be slightly smaller, with a fractionally shorter pile. The most obvious contrast between the two is that Kansu designs are normally articulated in blues and whites, often with small amounts of additional colour, rather than just different shades of blue (pl. 4). Saddle-rugs are usually associated more with Kansu than Suiyuan, although it is not always clear whether this is based on fact or convention (pls. 7, 8).

The term 'Kansu' is also applied, mainly by the Chinese, to East Turkestan rugs, which were often imported into China via Kansu. This can lead to confusion, and it is always advisable to enquire as to which category of rug the term is being applied. Fortunately, Chinese 'Kansus' and East Turkestan rugs marketed under the same name are totally dissimilar, and, with a little experience, there should be no difficulty in telling them apart.

In contemporary rugs, traditional Kansu designs are found primarily on items from the Antique Finish range, although they sometimes appear in a slightly modified form on Standard Chinese rugs. However, the name 'Kansu' is often applied to items from the Sinkiang range, which is based on old East Turkestan rugs (pls. 9, 10).

Paotao is the capital of Suiyuan province, and no doubt produced a number of classic Suiyuan rugs. However, dealers and collectors consider Paotao rugs to belong to a distinct category of their own. They are frequently large, sometimes very large, and employ richly coloured, naturalistic schemes. Landscapes and animals are the most common motifs (pl. 42), and they are often depicted through 'windows' or 'peepholes', which give the impression that a section has been cut out of a monochrome field and laid over part of a more extensive scene. Paotaos are generally finely knotted, with short piles, and use a broad palette of lush blues, reds, yellows and greens.

In contemporary rugs, traditional Paotao designs find their fullest expression in the Tapestry range (pls. 40, 41), but may also be found in Antique Finish and Standard Chinese rugs, although in the latter range, the colours are generally more subdued.

Ning-Hsia rugs (pl. 3) were originally made in the northern border town of Ning-Hsia (or Ning-Hsia Fu), which is situated in the province of the same name on the Chinese side of the Great Wall. Several authorities trace rug-making in Ning-Hsia back to the Ming Dynasty, and believe that it produced most of the carpets for the famous Stupa Temple (p. 49) and for other (mainly Tibetan) Buddhist temples and monasteries throughout China. These, and subsequent, Ning-Hsia rugs favoured Buddhist, Taoist and general mystical and mythological motifs and symbols, promoting long life, good fortune, happiness, fertility and career success, as well as more complex prophetic and philosophical messages. A wide range of other designs, ranging from dragons to flowers, may also be found, but the main distinguishing feature of Ning-Hsia rugs is considered to be their very high standard of manufacture and design.

In common with a number of other weaving centres, Ning-Hsia was strategically placed on an important trade route – in a triangular link between China, Tibet and Mongolia – and also served as a market-place for rugs produced, mainly by nomads, in the vast hinterland stretching into Mongolia. Consequently, rugs marketed in the town were also referred to as Ning-Hsias. In addition, Ning-Hsia gradually became synonymous with any well-made Chinese rug. It is therefore almost impossible, unless there is some undisputed provenance, to be absolutely sure whether a rug sold today as a Ning-Hsia was: a) made in the town, b) marketed in the town, or c) simply classified as a top quality Chinese rug by a dealer who wants to attract a higher price.

In contemporary rugs, old Ning-Hsia designs are found predominantly in the Antique Finish and, to a much lesser extent, Standard Chinese and Tapestry ranges.

Attribution and price are inextricably connected, and, although rugs are generally less affected by the 'cult of personality' than many other arts and crafts, collectors will frequently pay more if a rug is attributed to one group rather than another. Not surprisingly, dealers will often try to attribute rugs of uncertain origin to the weaving group that is currently commanding the highest price.

Rugs made during the reign of certain emperors are also deemed to be 'better quality', and thus more desirable and

expensive, than similar rugs produced during other periods. Consequently, rugs are often attributed to the reign of a specific emperor, rather than an approximate year: for example, the Chia Ch'ing period (*c.* 1796–1820), rather than *c.* 1800. This usually only applies to rugs made during the Ch'ing Dynasty (*c.* 1644–1911); anything older than this would generally be classified as Ming or late Ming, for example.

The Ch'ing emperors

Shun Chih (*c.* 1644–61)
K'ang Hsi (*c.* 1661–1722)
Yung Cheng (*c.* 1723–35)
Ch'ien Lung (*c.* 1736–96)
Chia Ch'ing (*c.* 1796–1820)
Tao Kuang (*c.* 1821–50)
Hsien Feng (*c.* 1851–61)
T'ung Chih (*c.* 1862–74)
Kuang Hsu (*c.* 1875–1908)
Hsuang T'ung (*c.* 1909–11)

The emperors' names used in this book are their 'reign names'; i.e. the name by which they were known when they were on the throne. It was normal practice for Chinese emperors to have four names: a) a personal name; b) a reign name; c) a temple, or religious, name; and d) a posthumous name, or *shih*, which was given to be used in the land of the Immortals.

East Turkestan rugs

The vast, mainly desert region traditionally known as East (or Chinese) Turkestan is believed by most authorities to be the cradle, if not the birthplace, of rug-making. The oldest known hand-knotted carpet, the Pazaryk (which has been dated to around the 5th century BC) was discovered during the excavation of a Scythian (or Turkoman) tomb, in 1949, on the Siberian side of the Altai mountains. The origins of this carpet, and almost everything surrounding it, remain a mystery and provide the subject

Bat and *shou* border of the Ch'ing Dynasty

for ongoing debate. Some authorities attribute the Pazaryk to Persia, while others argue that its discovery so far away from the Persian empire, coupled with the fact that the animal imagery found in its border is typical of early Scythian and Mongolian artists, make it more likely to be the work of nomadic weavers in Mongolia, or possibly the surrounding regions of Siberia, East Turkestan or Central Asia. However, regardless of the Pazaryk's exact origins, its presence in the region suggests that the techniques of hand-knotting were known, if not practised, here as early as the 1st millennium BC.

East Turkestan rugs, like the region from which they come, seem to possess an ability to absorb divers cultural and aesthetic elements, and yet still retain their own distinctive character. Their designs are basically Turkoman, and employ the same fusion of essentially Islamic and 'totemistic' motifs found in rugs from West Turkestan (incorporated into the former Soviet Union, Afghanistan and parts of northern Iran), but their colouring and overall 'mood' is fundamentally *Chinese*, with the predominant dark reds and blues being replaced by a more muted palette of gentler oranges, greens, browns and ochre yellows, as well as reds and blues.

Many classic Turkoman motifs have also undergone subtle transformations. For example, the round or slightly oval 'disk-forms', which are generally accepted as variants of the *gul* or 'medallion' motifs common to Turkoman and other *Persian/Islamic* rugs are clearly distinguished in East Turkestan rugs by the asymmetrical, slightly hazy manner of their articulation (pp. 10, 100 and pl. 9). This could, of course, simply be a sign of clumsiness on the part of the weaver, but the skill shown in other parts of these designs would seem to indicate a deliberate desire to produce a less rigid and symmetrical form, which, combined with the softer palette, produces a gentler, more meditative effect. Similarly, the 'pomegranate' design appears to be a variation of the Tree-of-Life scheme found in general Turkoman, Belouch and numerous other *Persian/Islamic* rugs; aesthet-

ically and symbolically, however, it seems closer to the *Chinese* notion of 'fertility' and 'abundance' (of which the pomegranate is a symbol), than to the more precise Islamic vision of a bridge linking Paradise to the world of men and the world below.

The distinctive nomadic character of East Turkestan rugs, as well as their more obvious use of Islamic symbolism, makes them clearly distinguishable from the majority of rugs from China proper (although a strong East Turkestan influence can be seen in some Chinese items, particularly from the border regions – e.g. Kansu and Ning-Hsia). However, they are often very similar to Mongolian weavings, and, although generally less brightly coloured, resemble some Tibetan rugs.

In contemporary rugs, East Turkestan designs are found almost exclusively in the Sinkiang (or Kansu) range (pls. 9, 10).

East Turkestan weaving groups are even more arbitrary than Chinese weaving groups, and derive their names from the major towns on the Silk Route where they were traditionally marketed. For centuries, nomadic weavers from all over East Turkestan sold their wares in Samarkand, Tashkent, Yarkand, Kashgar and Khotan, and, gradually, their rugs became known by the names of these marketing towns. In the West it was common practice to call all East Turkestan rugs 'Samarkands', because Samarkand, being the most westerly of these towns, was the place where they were gathered for transportation to Europe. In contrast, the Chinese referred to them collectively as 'Kansus', because Kansu province, which borders East Turkestan, was the entry point for their importation into China. At the beginning of the 20th century East Turkestan was divided between the USSR and China; Samarkand and Tashkent were incorporated into the USSR (contemporary East Turkestan-style rugs woven in the former Soviet Union are now marketed as 'Samarkands'), and Yarkand, Kashgar and Khotan became part of the People's Republic of China.

The names of these last three towns are now used to classify East Turkestan rugs. However, there is no concrete evidence to support the view that the rugs marketed in each of these towns were consistently different in style and character from those marketed elsewhere. In addition, there is often little uniformity in the criteria used by dealers and rug historians for assessing whether a rug originates from Kashgar, Yarkand or Khotan. For example, some dealers associate pomegranate designs with Kashgar; others attribute this scheme more to Khotan or Yarkand. Similarly, the central medallion, or *ay-gul*, scheme is associated by different authorities with each of the three weaving groups; and some argue that rugs employing this design should in fact be attributed to Kansu (China). It is therefore impossible to give a clear and consistently applied indication of the specific features associated with the rugs from each group, but the following are among the most frequently encountered.

Khotan (Hotan), the most easterly of the groups, is especially associated with *saph* designs (p. 99), similar to those produced in Kayseri, Turkey, and silk pieces, although some authorities also link it more with medallion and *ay-gul* schemes (pl. 9).

Kashgar, the most westerly of the groups, is often associated with 'pomegranate' schemes (pl. 10), especially those that employ delicate latticing, in addition to peony medallions (or *guls*) and other all-over floral and lattice designs.

Yarkand lies roughly midway between Khotan and Kashgar, and is often associated with pomegranate and *ay-gul*, as well as other typical East Turkestan designs. Some authorities believe that Yarkand rugs are woven in a slightly different manner to other East Turkestan rugs, but this has not been universally accepted.

Unattributed rugs from the region are normally marketed simply as East Turkestan rugs, although dealers will sometimes make an arbitrary attribution in the hope of securing a higher price.

Mongolian rugs

Mongolia, rather than East Turkestan, is believed by some authorities to be the birthplace of rug-making. Unfortunately, there is very little evidence to pinpoint when exactly Mongolian rugs were first made. Some rugs dating from the 13th century and others from the 18th and 19th centuries have been discovered, but, apart from one large carpet attributed to the 14th or 15th century (which some authorities believe could be Turkish or even European), we know of no authenticated Mongolian rugs from either earlier or intervening centuries. The Mongols, like most primarily nomadic people, possessed only the most rudimentary elements of written history, so most of the literary and pictorial evidence concerning their rugs is provided by other cultures, particularly the Chinese. Sung Dynasty paintings illustrating aspects of contemporary Mongol life, for example, confirm that rugs were in existence at the turn of the 1st millennium; and other fragments of evidence suggest that Mongol weaving is much older, dating back to at least the 3rd or 4th centuries AD.

Few authorities would dispute that pile-weaving in the region is both very old and, in common with other Central and Far East-Asian nomadic cultures, an important part of their artistic expression and way of life. Indeed, it would be extremely surprising if Mongolian nomads had not come into contact with their counterparts in East Turkestan, and if there had not been some exchange of skills such as rug-making, which were so obviously relevant to their mutual lifestyles. The more interesting speculation is perhaps who learned from whom.

Mongolian rugs also have much in common with Tibetan rugs, which is hardly surprising in view of the cultural and historical links between the two nations. In the 8th century AD the Tibetan empire stretched through East Turkestan and western China to the Mongolian border country, and Tibetan mercenaries played a significant part in the conquests of Genghis Khan and other Mongol leaders; the Tibetan and Mongolian peoples are also closely related both ethnically and linguistically. The similarity in their arts and crafts also leaves little room to doubt that mutual influence was at work.

In terms of rug-making, it seems probable that Mongolian weaving techniques and designs were first imported into Tibet, and then, in the 16th century, when Tibetan Buddhism was exported into Mongolia, Buddhist-inspired Tibetan designs found their way into Mongolian rugs. Certainly, there seem to be two distinct types, or groups, of Mongolian rugs:

Secular rugs (similar in design, though not in colour, to pls. 4, 7, 8) are the oldest and most common Mongolian weavings, and frequently employ geometric medallion-and-corner, or repeating designs, with fret, swastika, meander and stylized floral forms. The 13th-century Mongolian rugs (which are the oldest known) belong to this type, as do many of the items dating from the 18th and 19th centuries, and they possess the same overall characteristics as nomadic-style Tibetan and, to a much lesser extent, East Turkestan rugs, as well as some items produced in the border regions of China. These 'secular' items are usually either brightly coloured (far more than is usual in China or East Turkestan) or employ predominantly browns, whites and ochres; blue rarely features strongly in the Mongolian palette, probably because the indigo plant (from which blue is derived) is not as common in Mongolia as it is elsewhere. It seems highly probable that rugs of this type and design influenced the production of similar items in Tibet.

Religious rugs are those that incorporate Buddhist and other *Chinese* mystical and religious motifs. There is no evidence of this type of rug being produced in Mongolia much before the 18th century, and the general opinion is that these schemes were imported from Tibet, and China, some time after the 13th century, when Tibetan Buddhism was brought into the country. Although these 'religious' rugs appear to draw almost as much of their symbolism from China as from Tibet, their more vibrant colour schemes and bolder articulation of design make them closer in character to Tibetan rugs.

Mongolian weaving groups have never been classified, because there is not enough evidence regarding either where the rugs were made, or whether the weavers belonged to any clearly defined Mongol sub-tribes. Consequently, items made in Mongolia are marketed simply as Mongolian rugs.

In contemporary rugs, Mongolian designs may occasionally be found (usually in modified form) in rugs from the Chinese Antique Finish and, less frequently, Sinkiang ranges, as well as in some of the Authentic Tibetan rugs from Nepal.

Manchu rugs

There is little doubt that the Manchus, who were primarily nomadic, made and used rugs long before they conquered China and established the Ch'ing (or Manchu) Dynasty (*c.* 1644–1911), but we know almost nothing about the history of rug development in Manchuria. We do know that the Manchus not only brought both their rugs and their weaving skills into China, but also stimulated the rug-making industry (p. 49). However, during the course of their reign, a fusion gradually took place between Manchu and Chinese culture, and, although it is reasonable to speculate that some of the more 'nomadic'-style rugs, particularly those from the northern weaving centres, may be strongly Manchu in character, we cannot point to any groups of rugs that can be defined as exclusively Manchu in either origin or style.

Tibetan rugs

Tibet, as an ethnic and geographical entity, can be traced back to the Yarland kings of the 1st century BC, and almost certainly existed, probably in a more fragmented system of fiefdoms, much earlier. Lhasa, established as the Tibetan capital shortly after the turn of the 1st millennium, acted as the administrative centre for the advanced metalworking industries (mainly iron, copper, silver and gold) that flourished throughout the region. However, Song-tsen Gam-po (AD *c.* 618–49) is generally considered by the Tibetans to be the first monarch and founder of the country, and they date their history from his ascension to the throne.

The 'kingdom' founded by Song-tsen Gam-po lasted until the beginning of the 10th century, and during this period Tibet became one of the most powerful countries in Asia, expanding its empire into China, India and Burma, and engaging in an ongoing conflict with the T'ang emperors. After one successful Tibetan incursion into China, the T'ang emperor T'ai Tsung (c. 628–50) followed the time-honoured Chinese tradition of giving his daughter, the Princess Wen Chang, in marriage to his 'worthy rival' Song-tsen Gam-po. This piece of shrewd diplomacy did not prevent further Tibetan invasions of China, but it had a profound effect on the cultural and religious evolution of Tibet.

The Princess Wen Chang was one of the most impressive and influential figures in Tibetan history. Not only did she bring with her a retinue of Chinese artists and craftsmen, thus opening the door for cultural and artistic interchange between her native and adopted countries, she also brought a large bronze Buddha, known as the Jovo Rimpoche, which was believed to have been made in Magadha during Buddha's lifetime, and which is now one of the holiest of all Buddhist artefacts. Although Buddhism had been introduced two hundred years earlier, it is Wen Chang who is credited with her husband's conversion, and, in union with his other wife (a Nepalese Buddhist princess), with persuading him to reintroduce Buddha's teachings into Tibet.

Song-tsen Gam-po's successor, King Ti-song De-tsen (740–86), was a disciple of Tantric Buddhism, whose doctrines and beliefs seemed to strike a more sympathetic chord with the native Bon-po (followers of the ancient shamanistic Bon religion that dominated Tibet), and towards the end of his life he presided over a predominantly Buddhist kingdom. After the fall of the monarchy, in the 10th century, Tibet was effectively ruled by a series of priest/kings, who later adopted – on the death of dGe-dun-grub (c. 1394–1475) – a system of temporal and spiritual rulership based on a succession of 'reincarnated' Dalai Lamas.

The process of cultural exchange begun by King Song-tsen Gam-po continued until the 17th century. 'Newer' artists and craftsmen (Indianized people of Mongol descent), who can still be found in isolated colonies today, were originally introduced into Tibet from Nepal by Song-tsen Gam-po's Nepalese wife, and worked alongside the Chinese craftsmen imported by the Princess Wen Chang. Rugs were probably in use during this entire 'monarchical' period, but there is no clear evidence to indicate whether they were imported, made in Tibet, or a combination of both. We know that Tibet had earlier cultural links with the Sassanian Dynasty in Persia (c. 226–625), in addition to long-established contacts with India and Nepal, and it is certainly possible that rugs entered Tibet, either directly or indirectly, from one of these sources. Unfortunately, Tibetan records are almost non-existent for this period, and Chinese historians (from whom much of our knowledge of Tibet and Tibetan crafts have been gained) took very little notice of their neighbours until the 7th century, when the Tibetan kings began their conflict with the T'ang emperors. Rugs could also have been introduced into Tibet before the 7th century by East Turkestan and Mongolian nomads, but, in common with Tibet, these cultures possessed an essentially oral historical tradition, and so the only evidence available is from 'handed-down' folk tales, which cannot be taken as absolute proof.

From the 10th century onwards Tibet strengthened its ties with Mongol culture. Tibetan monks were responsible for converting Kublai Khan to Buddhism and introducing the religion into Mongolia, thereby consolidating the already strong affinity between the two peoples. Despite the lack of firm corroborating evidence, it is almost impossible to believe that Mongolian weaving was not introduced – or, quite possibly, reintroduced – during this period. The close cultural, ethnic and now religious bonds between the two peoples help to explain why the Mongols, despite conquering all of China and much of Asia, never attempted either to invade or obtain tribute from Tibet. For the first time in nearly a millennium, Tibet could feel reasonably secure from Chinese invasion; consequently, the period between the 11th and 15th centuries saw a continued development of Tibetan culture and art, including rug-making. However, from the 16th century onwards, Tibet became gradually caught between two equally destructive forces: growing Chinese political interference, and isolationism at home. From the 18th century, a combination of territorial claims and political interference by the Chinese pushed Tibet towards an even stricter policy of isolationism, culminating, in 1950, in the largely unopposed Chinese invasion and annexation of the country.

The origin of Tibetan rugs is a source of considerable debate and disagreement amongst carpet historians. Most argue that because Tibetan rugs are 'Chinese' in overall character and appearance, the techniques of rug-making must have been introduced from China. This argument, however, fails to take account of several important facts. First, the unique technique of Tibetan weaving (p. 29); when a foreign craft is incorporated into a culture, the usual pattern is to copy the technique, and then modify the designs to suit local modes of expression, rather than copy the designs and create a diametrically opposed technique. Second, many Tibetan rugs are not 'Chinese' in appearance, but more in keeping with those of Mongolia, East Turkestan and elsewhere. Third, rugs appear to have been in common use in Tibet centuries before any record of their use in China (although this cannot be proved either way). Fourth, the main centres of Tibetan rug-making were largely situated in the regions farthest away from China, rather than close to the border, where Chinese influence might be assumed to have been greatest. Fifth, it is quite clear that Tibet has had strong links with several other rug-making cultures – including Mongolia, East Turkestan, India and Persia – dating back to the beginning of the 1st millennium AD. Finally, and perhaps most importantly, the history of this part of Asia has been one of almost constant invasion, ethnic migration, trade and religious interchange, making it almost impossible for Tibetans to have remained ignorant of rug-making. This, coupled with the almost universal link between rugs and the nomadic way of life,

makes it more probable that rugs would have been readily adopted by the largely nomadic culture of Tibet than by the urbanized society of China proper.

We do not know who introduced rug-making into Tibet, or even if it developed there entirely independently, but it seems probable that rugs were first imported from East Turkestan, Central Asia, Mongolia or even Persia, and that the skills were either evolved gradually by trial and error (which would explain the Tibetans' unique weaving technique), or learned directly from migrant (probably nomadic) weavers belonging to one or more of the existing rug-making cultures. There is little doubt that Tibetan rugs were influenced by Chinese designs, but that is hardly surprising when one considers the broad similarity in religious and mythological beliefs throughout the Far East, and China's dominant position in the region.

In Tibet, rugs were used primarily as something on which to lie or sit – e.g. as seat covers, saddle covers, floor cushions and even beds – and were made in various shapes and sizes, many being given a specific name to denote their function (e.g. *masho*, a small oblong rug for putting on a wooden saddle, and *makden*, a similar one placed under a saddle). This way of using rugs is essentially nomadic, compatible with Mongol, East Turkestan and Manchu lifestyles, and opposite to the primary Chinese usage of rugs as floor coverings. Most of our knowledge regarding the organization of weaving in Tibet dates from the 18th and 19th centuries, and we can only speculate about how exactly this evolved, but it is clear that there were three distinct, although probably overlapping, groups – each catering for its own general market – which can be classified loosely as nomadic, peasant and commercial.

Nomadic rugs were woven by nomads primarily for their own use – although some were undoubtedly sold to the settled population – and generally consisted of relatively small, coarsely knotted, brightly coloured rugs, saddle covers and other woven artefacts. The second group were made in individual households, again primarily for their own use, although richer families would often buy their rugs from, or employ full-time, the better local weavers. In common with nomadic rugs, these items were usually fairly coarsely knotted and brightly coloured, but were frequently larger and slightly more refined, especially those commissioned or made for sale. Commercial weaving was still largely based on a 'cottage-industry' model, employing small groups of weavers in urban or semi-urban centres, but the rugs produced in these workshops were far more sophisticated, and were destined for the vast religious and, to a lesser extent, nobility markets at home and abroad.

Tibetan weaving groups follow the same arbitrary pattern of classification as Chinese weaving groups, and can be broadly divided between those in 'Tibet proper' and 'cultural Tibet'. It is important to stress, however, that the following groups are broad classifications made on the basis of a general regional style, and, unless there is a clear provenance, it is advisable to remain sceptical about attributions to any of these specific groups.

Tibetan rugs are normally marketed simply as 'Tibetan', so the problem of specific attributions rarely applies, but it is almost certain that if one weaving group were suddenly to come into vogue and begin commanding higher prices, some dealers would undoubtedly try everything in their power to obtain evidence pointing to the fact that 'their' rugs belong to that group.

Central Tibetan rugs are generally very well made, fairly sophisticated in appearance and were produced in a wide variety of sizes and shapes. Their colour schemes are typically rich and vivid, without being garish, and feature a broad range of Tibetan and Tibetanized Chinese designs. They are often divided into sub-groups, based on the styles associated with the weaving areas around the towns of Lhasa, Shigatse and Gyantse, from which they draw their names. (Similar to pls. 7, 8.)

Kampa Dzong rugs are associated with an area in southern Tibet leading to Sikkim, in India, which is dominated by large castles (*dzong*) built to guard against Nepalese raiders. These items are coarsely knotted on woollen warps and wefts, and employ extremely vivid colours and relatively simple geometric designs (similar to pl. 30). They are nevertheless extremely attractive examples of 'peasant' weaving (sometimes referred to as the Tso-rug style).

Gya-rum is the name given to a group of high quality rugs with very strong Chinese characteristics (similar to pls. 3, 33). The word *gya* means 'expanse' (*gya-kar*, the white expanse, is the Tibetan name for India; *gya-nag*, the black expanse, is the name for China), but it is unclear whether the name refers to their coming *from* the 'expanse' (China), or whether it was applied later, when the Manchu emperors imported them into China. They are generally far more sophisticated, and larger, than most other Tibetan rugs, and were found almost exclusively in important monasteries and the homes of the very rich.

Border rugs are made in the Amdo and Kham regions of cultural Tibet, which, despite overwhelming Tibetan populations, have long been a disputed buffer zone between Tibet and China. Two broad styles of rug emanate from this region. The first includes rugs with very strong Chinese characteristics (although they are woven using Tibetan methods), and there is an ongoing debate as to whether they are Tibetan copies of Chinese originals, or Tibetan rugs in styles later adopted by the Chinese (similar to pl. 38). The second group are coarsely woven, brightly coloured, peasant-style rugs (like Kampa Dzong rugs) with mainly geometric and stylized floral motifs (similar to pls. 28, 29).

Ladakh, Sikkim, Nepal and Bhutan had minor rug-weaving industries based around Tibetan settlers and nomads (similar to pl. 37), but very little is known about specific regional characteristics. The assumption is that weaving was largely confined to nomads and a few settled 'peasant' weavers who produced rugs mainly for themselves; and that more sophisticated items for aristocratic and monastic use, were imported directly from Tibet. However, these countries play an important part in contemporary Tibetan weaving.

Chapter VII

Contemporary rugs

Rug-making in China and the Chinese sphere of influence has changed dramatically during the course of the 20th century. Some traditional weaving countries have ceased to produce rugs altogether, or produce them in such small quantities (almost exclusively for domestic use) that they must now be largely discounted, even as minor rug-making entities. Some have been physically absorbed into other nations, and the individuality of their rugs has been lost.

However, in contrast to this general decline, China and Nepal have both turned what was a relatively minor domestic craft into a vast and extremely profitable export business. China has steadily increased its share of the world market since the 1970s, and, if current trends continue (and they show no signs of abating), it will be the world's single largest supplier of handmade oriental rugs by the turn of the century. Nepal may not be able to compete with China in terms of volume, but, for a country that barely had a carpet industry before the 1960s, its development is impressive. By the time of the Hanover (Domotex) Fair in 1990, handmade rugs had become Nepal's largest single export and earner of foreign currency. Today, when dealers talk of contemporary *Chinese* rugs, they are normally referring to items produced in these two countries. Small pockets of production exist elsewhere, but the vast majority of handmade *Chinese* rugs, particularly those exported to the West, are made in either China or Nepal.

Chinese rugs

The growing popularity of Chinese rugs is based partly on their traditional character and appearance, and partly on the ability of China's carpet industry to adapt to changing market demands while maintaining the highest standards of quality and quality control. This adaptability has given the Chinese rug-making industry a distinct commercial advantage over most of its competitors. India and Pakistan have both successfully adapted their designs and colour schemes to conform to Western taste, but neither can offer the same variety of individual ranges – each with its own unique characteristics and repertoire of designs – as the Chinese. Nor are they able to compete in the expanding 'contract' and 'programmed continuity line' markets, in which customers' own compositions can be produced quickly and relatively inexpensively (p. 136). Most other producing countries operate similar systems, but the Chinese can make to order a rug of any size, quality, colour and design, within a specified period for the agreed price. In short, the Chinese run their rug-making industry as a highly competitive business, which caters to the demands of a number of external markets, rather than combining a commercial, 'export-earning' business with a desire to preserve and promote a traditional, and historically precious, national craft – as is still the case, for example, in Turkey and Iran.

The quality control of Chinese carpets is exceptional, and even their most passionate detractors admit that the consistency of Chinese rugs, coupled with the clear identification of each different individual quality, or grade, sets them apart from rugs produced elsewhere. For example, there may be little to choose in terms of technical quality between a Persian (Iranian) 'Nain' and a Chinese version of a 'Nain' design – and most authorities would probably argue that the Persian rug is normally aesthetically superior. But a top grade (e.g. 240-line) Chinese version, with very few exceptions, will always be of the same technical quality, whereas a Persian Nain may vary from excellent to mediocre, without any clear, external indication of where it belongs within the range. Consequently, the only criteria for assessing the quality of a Persian rug are personal judgment and the general reputation of the particular weaving group, coupled with any assurances the seller may give. In contrast, buying a Chinese rug leaves little to chance; even rugs with the same basic designs are clearly defined in terms of quality, and the buyer knows not only that a 240-line item is technically superior to a 160-line item, but also that all 240-line rugs will be of exactly the same structural, and usually aesthetic, merit.

The background to modern production

Before examining in detail the development of contemporary rugs, it is important to look at the transition from the old system of manufacture to the beginning of modern production. As with most changeovers, the process was gradual, and it is impossible to fix an exact date when one system ended and the other began. However, it is generally accepted that the era of old, or traditional, Chinese rugs drew to a close some time around the fall of the Ch'ing Dynasty, in 1911, while the contemporary rug-making industry was established shortly after the Chinese Revolution, in 1949. The intervening years saw a slow metamorphosis in both the methods and aims of rug production, and the rugs made during this 'transitional' period possess their own distinct characteristics, which span both the old and the new.

These changes can probably be traced back to the mid-19th century, when the West began to have an increasing influence on Chinese society as a whole (p. 118), although the full impact of Western influence on rug-making did not become apparent until just after the turn of the century. No one can be absolutely certain exactly when, or why, the West turned its attention to Chinese rugs, but it is generally accepted that the invasion of China by European troops, in 1900, to quell the so-called Boxer Rebellion (a nationalist uprising against Western interference in Chinese affairs), was the critical event. Thousands of soldiers and commercial interests looted the imperial palaces, treasure-houses and museums, as well as private dwellings, and returned home with their booty – which included Chinese rugs.

Some of these found their way into the hands of a small number of serious collectors, mainly in the United States, and, within a few years, Chinese rugs, which had hitherto been dismissed as 'shoddy' and 'inferior' by the majority of dealers, suddenly started to become fashionable. This vogue for Chinese rugs increased during the First World War (no doubt partly assisted by Turkey's involvement in the conflict and the subsequent difficulty in importing their, and other Middle Eastern, rugs), and was given a further seal of approval shortly afterwards when *New Country Life* (later *Country Life*), *House Beautiful* and other American lifestyle magazines began to promote 'all things Chinese'. Around this time, a number of American and other Western importers (e.g. A. Beshar and Co., Karagheusian, and the Asian Rug and Trading Co.) established

Bat, fret and floral border

offices in China, and sent their own people to supervise the weaving of 'their' rugs. The economic boost to the Chinese rug-making industry by this sudden Western (especially American) investment had a dramatic impact on both the level and the focus of production, leading to a standardization of manufacture and an emphasis on satisfying export demands.

The two most important and far-reaching effects of this were: a) the integration of Western and Chinese designs, and b) the foetal development of ranges. Western designs quickly became established as part of the Chinese repertoire, and a number of rugs based on a mixture of French (Aubusson and Savonnerie), Spanish and Persian compositions, with traditional Chinese tonal and thematic schemes, were made for export to Europe and North America. Some rugs were even made to conform totally to Western designs. The highly collectable Fette rugs, for example, designed by Mrs Helen Fette, featured a variety of Chinese and Spanish motifs in the pastel colours usually associated with 17th-century French rugs. Beshar and Co. took this trend a stage further and commissioned one hundred rugs designed with symbols of American 'Ivy League Schools' for sale to students and alumni.

The concept of ranges was not fully incorporated into Chinese weaving until after the Revolution, in 1949. However, the majority of rugs produced in the 1920s were classified as belonging to either the 'Peking' or 'Tientsin' styles associated with workshops operating in those towns. Rugs were also produced in a number of other places – most notably Kalgan, Yulin, Tatung and Shanghai – but, with few exceptions, these items are indistinguishable from those made in Peking or Tientsin. The most influential importing nations during this period (in descending order) were the United States, Japan, Great Britain and Canada, and the majority of importers from

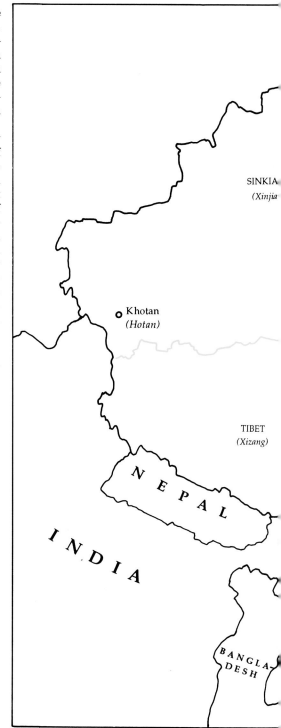

The provinces of modern China. Where appropriate, the *pinyin* name is given in parentheses below the Wade-Giles version

MONGOLIA

HEILONGJIANG

KIRIN
(Jilin)

Haerpin
(Harbin)

LIAONING

HEXI CORRIDOR

Paotou
(Baotou)

INNER MONGOLIA
(Nei Monggol)

Peking
(Beijing)

HOPEH
(Hebei)

TIENTSIN
(Tianjing)

SHANSI
(Shanxi)

SHANTUNG
(Shandong)

TSINGHAI
(Qinghai)

NINGHSIA

KANSU
(Gansu)

SHENSI
(Shaanxi)

HONAN
(Henan)

KIANGSU
(Jiangsu)

AHWEI
(Anhui)

SZECHUAN
(Sichuan)

HUBEI

Wuhan

CHINKIANG
(Zhenjiang)

KIANGSI
(Jiangxi)

HUNAN

FUKIEN
(Fujian)

JTAN

KWECHOU
(Guizhou)

FORMOSA
(Taiwan)

YUNNAN

KWANGSI
(Guangsi)

KWANTUNG
(Guangdong)

Canton
(Guangzhou)

BURMA

these countries had close ties with one of the two main weaving centres, and exercised strong control over the rugs produced, including their overall character and repertoire of designs. Consequently, the contrasting styles and qualities of Peking and Tientsin rugs were largely influenced by the criteria laid down by each importing company, which were in turn dictated by the demands of the 'specific' market at which the rugs were aimed.

Peking workshop rugs, which were produced in a number of workshops in Peking, and probably elsewhere, were largely based on much older, traditional Chinese designs. They were referred to (in China) as 'Palace Style' rugs, because they specialized, at least initially, in emulating the rug schemes found in imperial palaces, temples, and the homes of the nobility and more affluent families. Their colours were typically Chinese, with subtle shades of blue, yellow, buff, white and gold, and their favourite designs were small central medallions, often with bats or flowers, set against a sparsely decorated field. In addition, they produced a number of pictorial rugs, and items with a mixture of Taoist, Buddhist and Confucian designs.

The fact that they were based on traditional rugs, however, did not stop the Peking workshops from developing their own individual characteristics, and producing, for example, a number of items featuring symbolically powerful five-clawed, or imperial, dragons (which had been banned during the Ch'ing Dynasty except in rugs made for the emperor) as an act of retrospective defiance (similar to pl. 2). They also used their new-found freedom of expression to break other compositional taboos.

The Western importers associated with Peking workshops (like Tadcross and Co., for whom the Kai Yuan rug factory manufactured items exclusively from 1920 to 1949) generally wanted good quality rugs in more or less authentic colours and designs for sale to their slightly more sophisticated and overtly 'Sinophile' markets. The fortunes of the Peking workshops began to wane in the mid- to late 1920s, when the

Western (particularly American) fashion for *chinoiserie* declined, and the demand became increasingly for the cheaper, more Westernized Tientsin rugs.

Tientsin workshop rugs were produced in dozens of workshops in Tientsin and elsewhere, and were aimed primarily at the mass markets of North America and Europe, which wanted cheap handmade rugs in more Western colours and designs. Consequently, items were produced either in overtly Western schemes (such as Aubusson) or in predominantly Westernized Chinese designs. Tientsin workshop rugs generally featured asymmetrical compositions involving naturalistic floral, bird, tree, vase, boat and pagoda motifs, usually set in diagonally opposing corners against an open or sparsely decorated field. Occasionally, a central motif was employed, although medallions were rare, and many items had only plainly coloured, or sometimes no, borders. The colour schemes were often decided by the client, and many featured such un-Chinese hues as burgundy, burnt orange, green, purple, mauve and turquoise. After the fashion for *chinoiserie* declined in the West, Tientsin rugs became increasingly popular as cheap handmade items that could be produced to satisfy changing Western decorative tastes while still possessing an exotic Chinese flavour (similar to pls. 17, 18).

The collectability of Peking and Tientsin workshop rugs is a matter for personal judgment. Many rug dealers and historians consider them to be inferior examples of rug-making, with some curiosity value but little aesthetic or technical merit. However, this was the opinion held by most people in the carpet business about Chinese rugs in general until they began to draw an increasing number of collectors in the 1970s; it would be very surprising if Peking rugs in particular – belonging as they do to such a distinct and critical formative era – did not sooner or later become as collectable as other older Chinese rugs.

The Communist era
The Japanese invasion of China, in 1937, decimated the already declining rug-

making industry, and it was not until its re-organization under the new Communist regime, in the early 1950s, that its fortunes improved. In 1953 a series of 'five-year plans' was initiated, in an attempt to transform China from an agrarian into an industrial nation, including one aimed at revitalizing the rug industry. A number of small collectives, known as Carpet Producers' Co-operatives, were established and gradually developed into state-owned and -controlled workshops and manufactories. By the early 1970s a number of additional centres had come into operation, as Chinese rugs had once again begun to make an impact on Western markets.

The commercial and marketing strategies of the Communist industry were based on those pioneered by the Peking and Tientsin workshops at the beginning of the century. The idea was to produce reasonably cheap, decent quality rugs, catering for a broad range of mainly European and North American decorative tastes, and destined primarily for these export markets. In order to achieve this, the rug-making industry revived the concept of standard ranges, with a built-in 'design flexibility' that would enable them to adapt, expand or replace any of their ranges, and, by extension, to produce items of any size, shape, colour or design, on demand.

The organization of rug-making in China is split between several government bureaucracies, distribution centres and provincial workshop networks, all of which have a history of competing for higher levels of control. Overall policy coordination, including pricing, standards, exports and sales, is vested in the China Native Produce and Animal By-Produce Import and Export Corporation, in Peking (Beijing). However, the actual manufacture of rugs is under the control of the Ministry of Light Industry, also in Peking, who devolve their responsibility for local production to regional branches of the Arts and Crafts Industry Corporation.

Rugs are currently produced in twenty-three provinces, municipalities and autonomous regions, and distributed through export agencies in Peking, Tientsin, Darien, Shanghai, Tsingtao and, more recently, Sinkiang, Hopei, Zhejiang, Jiangsu and Kansu. However, as the scale and variety of Chinese rugs continue to increase, the number of both production and distribution centres is likely to expand.

There is no clearly defined and consistent correlation between the ranges, qualities and styles of contemporary Chinese rugs and the local weaving centres in which they are made. However, some regions and broad geographical areas (e.g. Sinkiang) tend to specialize in specific ranges or styles. Similarly, certain workshops, regardless of their location, may specialize in certain ranges, styles or qualities either because of easy access to particular distribution networks (e.g. proximity to silk-producing centres), or simply because they have geared themselves, in terms of skill and equipment, to concentrate on those types of rug.

The Chinese rug ranges

Shortly after the Chinese Revolution, the rug-making industry develped four ranges, or overall styles of rug, which were known as: Esthetic (Aubusson, pl. 21), Peking (traditional, pls. 15, 22), Floral and Self-tone (embossed or sculptured); all were loosely based on the types and styles produced by the Peking and Tientsin workshops earlier this century. These initial ranges have subsequently been modified and extended, as part of an ongoing response to market forces, and today there are a number of clearly defined ranges, in addition to items that are either made to order or part of an 'experimental' or 'minor interest' line.

The ranges outlined below illustrate the broadly defined stylistic and technical groupings of contemporary Chinese rugs. They should not, however, be considered as synonymous with separate weaving groups. It should also be remembered that the organization of the Chinese rug-making industry makes absolute divisions impossible; some of the individual ranges discussed may be divided into additional ranges, or sub-ranges, and totally new, or hybrid, ranges may spring up from time to time. However, the classifications employed below should serve as a useful and valid guide.

A range can be defined as a group of rugs having an overall style and character, with a unifying repertoire of designs, colours and tonal schemes, as well as uniform structural standards in terms of quality, knotting, pile length, materials, sizes, shapes and finish. Rugs of corresponding quality within the same range should normally be the same price.

The Standard Chinese range (pls. 16–18, 21) is loosely based on the Western and Westernized Chinese designs pioneered in Tientsin workshop rugs, and is the range with which most people are familiar. These rugs are found in many department stores and are normally distinguished by their pastel colouring, boldly articulated, often floral-inspired, designs and thick, lustrous pile. Central medallions are a common feature in either Aubusson or more traditional Chinese formats, with variations of floral, *shou*, bat or other symbolic inner forms (pls. 21, 22). Alternatively, they may employ floral, animal, bird, Buddhist, Taoist or other motifs as corner decorations set against an open or sparsely decorated field (pl. 16). Other items within this range use panelled or repeating designs, and it has become quite common for black or dark blue to be used as a ground colour, although usually in conjunction with more pastel shades.

These rugs are produced in a number of standard sizes, including runners and circular, semi-circular and oval shapes. They are generally well made, durable and luxurious, with a slight lustre given to the pile. The most popular and best quality grade within this range is the 90-line closed-back, with a ⅝″ (16mm) pile, but other grades are also of excellent quality. In addition, reasonable quality silk rugs, including runners, are made in a similar repertoire of designs (pls. 17, 18). They are not particularly finely knotted, by silk-weaving standards, and the silk is rather coarse, but they can be very attractive and are undoubtedly excellent value for money.

Standard Chinese woollen rugs are marketed under a number of names, including 'Superwashed Chinese', 'Superwashed Peking or Tientsin', or simply Chinese, Peking or Tientsin. Items with classic Aubusson, or other floral, medallions may be referred to collectively as 'Aubusson'. They may also be named after their design (e.g. a dragon, *shou* or peony rug), or even after any likely sounding Chinese district or town. Silk-pile rugs are even less consistently marketed, and may be referred to as either silk Chinese, Peking, Tientsin or even Aubusson (depending on the design), or alternatively be named after a principal weaving centre (e.g. Hubei, Wuhan, Hopeh), which may or may not indicate where the rugs were actually made.

It is more important to check the grade, or quality, of items within this range than in any other, not only because the different grades look almost identical from the front, but also because vastly inferior tufted rugs (p. 135) employ many of the same designs.

The following grades are found in this range:

Woollen-pile rugs: a) Closed-back, 90-line, ⅝″ pile; 80-line, ⅝″ pile; and 70-line, ⅜″ and ⅜″ pile. b) Open-back, 90-line, ⅜″ and ⅜″ pile; 80-line, ⅝″ pile; 70-line, ⅜″ pile and ⅜″ pile.

Silk-pile rugs: on silk (warps and wefts) within this range are normally produced in a 120-line grade, with ⅜″ or ⅜″ piles, although the pile length seems to vary more than in woollen rugs.

The Sinkiang range (pls. 9, 10) is based on the old rugs of East Turkestan, and is the only contemporary Chinese range to be made exclusively in the region (Sinkiang province) traditionally associated with its style of rugs. The vast majority of designs are copies, or variations, of classic East Turkestan rugs, although some may be more akin to traditional Kansu or even Mongolian schemes, and are usually woven to give them the slightly 'rough-hewn' nomadic character of the originals; this is frequently emphasized by the use of an antique wash to emulate the effects of age.

The most common designs are pomegranate and allover lattice schemes, as well as medallions and repeating stylized floral motifs, but other compositions, including *saphs* and prayer rugs (p. 99), may also be found. Their colour schemes frequently employ the more traditional East Turkestan palette of reds, oranges, ochres, yellows, blues and browns, but it is possible to find them in more pastel tones, and also in different shades of grey or brown. They are normally produced in only one grade (110/120-line), but are available in a variety of sizes and shapes; runners are especially common, and a number of square items are also found.

Sinkiang rugs are generally well made, using good quality (often local) wool, and are amongst the most authentic and traditional in appearance of all contemporary Chinese rugs. They may be marketed under a number of different names, but Sinkiangs, Kansus (or Gansus) and Samarkands are the most common (although this last name is usually reserved for East Turkestan-style rugs produced in what was the Soviet Union). Alternatively, they may be named after one of the traditional East Turkestan weaving groups (i.e. Khotan, Kashgar or Yarkand).

Woollen-pile rugs: Open-back, 110/120-line, $\frac{3}{8}$" pile, either unwashed or with an antique wash.

The Antique Finish range (pls. 12–14) is based on the designs and general characteristics of old Chinese rugs. The majority of contemporary rugs are direct copies of old Peking schemes, but traditional Paotao, Suiyuan, Ning-Hsia and Kansu compositions may also be found. The dominant colours are blues, whites and creams, but a wide range of other traditional colours (e.g. yellows, reds, buff and greens) are also used. They are made predominantly in Inner Mongolia and northern China, using mainly local (*HoXi*) wool, and sometimes employ vegetable dyes. The distinguishing characteristic of Antique Finish rugs is their 'authenticity', in both structure and appearance, and their success in achieving this can be gauged by the fact that dealers and carpet historians have been known, on occasion, to mistake contemporary items for the antique originals on which they are based. Antique Finish rugs are normally produced in only one grade (100-line) in a

number of standard sizes, although runners and large carpets are rare, and they are usually marketed simply as Antique Finish rugs, or under the name of the traditional weaving group (e.g. Peking, Paotao, Suiyuan, Ning-Hsia, Kansu) associated with the design on which they are based.

Woollen-pile rugs: Open-back, 100-line, $\frac{3}{8}$" pile.

The Tapestry range (pls. 40–1) consists of rugs that are hand-knotted, in the same way as other carpets, but employ a slightly modified technique, whereby the individual pile yarns are made up of different-coloured threads; this serves to imbue the design with a more subtle, painterly quality. Tapestries are also very finely knotted, employing the equivalent of 260-lines upwards on most schemes; and the 'mixed-yarn' technique, because of its ability to impart shades or tonal grading, gives the impression of even finer knotting. The designs in this range are almost exclusively pictorial, and are either based on old Chinese (mainly Paotao) rugs, or drawn directly from other Chinese artistic sources (such as watercolours); occasionally, more Westernized, mainly animal, depictions can be found.

Scenes may be drawn from mythology (e.g. Shou Shan, the hills of longevity), legend and folklore (e.g. genii at the court of Si Wang Mu), or show historical and cultural events (e.g. the dragon-boat festival). Alternatively, the designs may be simply landscapes, animals or scenes from everyday life – although even the most apparently mundane Chinese representations often contain some spiritual or mythological intent (pl. 40).

The artistic and technical standards of the finer items in this range are remarkable, and, aided by the rich and varied palette of blues, reds, yellows, purples and greens, this is an area where weaving can be said to merge with the better examples of representational art. However, the less finely knotted items are not as impressive, and often border on kitsch, although they are rarely as vulgar and unattractive as Persian, or other Islamic, pictorial novelty rugs.

Tapestries are produced in both wool and silk in a variety of shapes and sizes, although very large items are rare, and are usually marketed as either tapestries or pictorial rugs. There are no clearly defined grades in the Tapestry range; both woollen- and silk-pile rugs start at around 260-line quality, usually with a $^2/_8''$ or $^3/_8''$ pile, and some items may reach 400 lines or more.

The Persian-design range (pl. 24) is one of the more recent innovations, and is based on the designs and physical structure of top quality Persian workshop rugs. The knotting and general structure are almost indistinguishable from the Persian originals, and the designs are mainly direct copies of schemes used by some of the major contemporary Persian weaving groups, especially Isfahan, Nain, Kashan and Quoom, and, to a lesser degree, Tabriz, Sarouk and Kerman. They employ the same rich but subtle Persian palette, with dominant blues, reds, creams and ochres, in addition to more pastel shades, and use a wide variety of classic medallion-and-corner, vase, Shah Abbas, Tree-of-Life, and other traditional *Persian/Islamic* designs.

Rugs employing the same, or very similar, designs may be produced with either wool or silk piles, and some items use a mixture of wool and silk in the pile. The general quality of the materials, as well as the level of craftsmanship, are of the highest standard, and, in a purely technical sense, Chinese Persian-design rugs are the equals of Persian originals. In fact, they often have a distinct advantage when it comes to consistency and quality control.

Chinese Persian-design rugs are produced in a wide variety of sizes and grades, and are normally considerably cheaper than Persian equivalents, although the relative prices in individual countries are largely dependent on the respective import tariffs and other importation costs. As a general rule, the more finely knotted items (200-line plus) are the most aesthetically successful, because the clarity of form needed to do justice to the intricate, curvilinear designs is often not possible in lower-grade items, which may appear slightly fuzzy and dull. Persian-design rugs may be marketed as

such, or under a number of names, including Chinese- or Sino-Nains, Isfahans, Kashans, or be named after one of the major Chinese weaving centres, which may or may not be where the rug was made.

Woollen-pile rugs: a) Open-back, $^2/_8''$ pile, in 100-line, 120-line, 150/160-line (the most popular lower grade items), 180-line, 200/210-line (the most popular medium to higher grade items), 240-line, 260-line and 300-line.

Silk-pile rugs: b) Open-back, $^2/_8''$ pile, in 260-line, 300-line, 360-line, 400-line.

Wool-and-silk pile rugs: c) Open-back, $^2/_8''$ pile, 200-line, 260-line (the most popular), 300-line.

Such is the flexibility of the Chinese rug-making industry that certain grades may be dropped, and others added, from time to time in order to test market response.

The Tibetan-design range (pl. 26) is made in a number of centres throughout China (not Tibet, although this may change as the political conflicts ease) and is loosely based on traditional Tibetan rugs. However, many of these designs are heavily Westernized, and the vast majority of Chinese 'Tibetan-range' rugs bear only a passing resemblance to Tibetan originals. They are woven using basic Chinese, rather than Tibetan, knotting techniques, and in overall character and appearance are similar to items from the Standard Chinese range. Medallions, repeating geometric and floral motifs, usually set against open or sparsely decorated fields, are the most popular compositions. The motifs are normally quite bold in their articulation, and are frequently set against a limited palette of pastel shades. Tibetan-design rugs are not particularly finely knotted, but they are well made, using good quality wool, and make attractive and durable furnishing items. They are usually referred to as Tibetan, or Chinese Tibetan, rugs; but may also be marketed under alternative names based loosely on their designs or on a traditional Tibetan weaving centre.

Woollen-pile rugs: Open-back, $^5/_8''$ pile, in 50-line, 60-line and 80-line.

Kelims (pl. 19), or flatweaves, are produced in a wide variety of designs, colours and sizes. They are well made, using good quality local wool, and often feature very Westernized floral schemes. Although they can be produced in large sizes and employ almost any pile rug design, the general tendency is for smaller, brightly coloured items in geometric or floral schemes. Kelims are not usually divided into grades.

Needlepoint and petit point ranges (pl. 20) are totally Western in both concept and execution. The Chinese have simply taken this traditional European and North American craft, and employed their abundant weaving skills in related fields to make a commercially viable product.

Needlepoint can be produced to order in any quality, size, shape, colour or design, including cushions, and the range of items on the market at any given time is often the result of particular lines being promoted by leading furnishing outlets in the importing countries. However, certain standard qualities, sizes and designs are generally available; these are usually relatively small – e.g. 3′ × 3′ (0.9 × 0.9 m) or 6′ × 4′ (1.8 × 1.2 m) – and often feature floral, or floral panelled, designs. The standard quality is 10-point (i.e. 10 stitches per inch), and the design is articulated in wool on cloth, generally cotton; the back is usually covered by an additional, mainly cotton, backing.

Petit point can also be produced in any quality, size, shape, colour or design, but the tendency is for smaller items employing more naturalistic floral designs. The standard quality uses 10-point stitching on the background design and 24-point (i.e. 24 stitches per inch), or more, on the individual motifs. Wool is used to articulate both the background and the individual motifs on a cloth, usually cotton, foundation; a similar material is normally used to cover the back.

These items are generally marketed simply as needlepoints or petit points.

The goat-wool range has not, as yet, made a significant impact on Western markets. These items are produced primarily in Shantung province, and, although lacking the lustre and more luxurious qualities of sheep's-wool carpets, are nevertheless extremely firm, heavy, durable and com-

paratively cheap. The designs and colour schemes are frequently less sophisticated versions of those found in the Standard Chinese range, and they are usually produced in an 80-line quality. They may be marketed as Chinese goat-wool rugs or as Shantungs (Shandongs). Alternatively they may derive their name from their design or from any plausible Chinese weaving centre.

Tufted rugs (similar to pls. 21, 22) are produced in a number of weaving centres throughout China, although they are most closely associated with Tientsin, and provide a functional alternative to genuine hand-knotted rugs. They are similar in appearance to rugs from the Standard Chinese range (with which they are often confused) and employ the same designs, colours, yarn, washing and sculpting. However, they are not hand-knotted (p. 28), and lack both the aesthetic integrity and long-term durability of genuine hand-knotted rugs. Because hand-tufting can be done so much faster than hand-knotting, they are considerably cheaper; and, although many carpet dealers dismiss them as being totally unworthy of consideration, they are nevertheless perfectly acceptable furnishing items, and are frequently better value than comparable (woollen-pile) machine-made alternatives.

Because of the cost and quality differentials between tufted and hand-knotted rugs, it is important to be able to distinguish between the two. This is easily done by looking at the back of the rug; if it has a cloth backing, it is almost certainly a tufted, not a hand-knotted rug.

Tufted rugs are also known as 'latex-backed', 'full-cuts' and 'gun-tufted' rugs, but they are not always marketed as such, and retail outlets, especially department stores, frequently fail to make a clear distinction between these and genuine hand-knotted items. Consequently, they are often marketed as Chinese, Washed-Chinese (although rarely 'Superwashed'), Tientsin, Peking or Aubusson rugs, but other names based on their designs or Chinese weaving centres may also be used. These rugs are not usually graded.

Contract rugs and continuity lines are the names most commonly used to describe the system of 'made to order' and 'mix and match' rug-making. The division between 'contract rugs' and 'continuity lines' is always slightly blurred, and at times quite arbitrary, but might best be defined in terms of scope. Contract rugs are literally 'rugs made to contract', and, in theory, the Chinese weaving industry will make a rug of any size, shape, quality, material, colour or design, to the client's specifications. For example, one could order a needlepoint in a Persian design, or a tapestry version of the Mona Lisa, or a 30′ (9 m)-long silk runner composed in a repeating ancestral 'coat of arms' design. In practice, however, these extremely individualistic specifications for rugs are rare, and the more general practice is for a set of samples to be sent to a client, which will show different styles, qualities, colours and designs. The client can then 'mix and match', choosing, for example, the design from one sample and asking for it to be woven in the colour scheme of another sample and the quality of a third.

Continuity lines are a refinement of this 'mix and match' procedure, whereby the major importers carry a large stock of rugs in the most popular combinations of colour and design. This enables retailers to carry a much more limited stock, which they can use to illustrate the rug's overall quality and style; their customers can look through a sample book or catalogue, showing a fuller range of colour schemes and designs, and make their choice. The retailer can then order the item, which should be in the importer's warehouse, and deliver it to the customer within a few days. This system is not exclusive to the Chinese – India, for example, has operated a similar programme for years – but China's ability to offer reliable deliveries at contracted prices has brought it to the forefront of the continuity line market.

There are an almost endless number of permutations in the number of ranges, or sub-ranges, that can be provided by these methods. The majority of contract and continuity-line items are simply variations of the qualities, colours and designs offered in the standard ranges. However, this system has generated some small but nevertheless significant additional ranges.

Art Deco and Art Nouveau rugs, for example, are now being produced in a 120-line quality, and have already made some impact on small sections of the export market. They are made to the usual Chinese standards of technical excellence, and, if the fashion for these styles continues, are likely to be re-launched as a new and distinctive range, offering a wider variety of qualities, sizes, colours and designs.

Tibetan rugs

Tibet is a civilization in exile, whose entire national, religious and cultural integrity is preserved by pockets of refugees living in foreign lands. The ten years following the Chinese invasion of Tibet, in 1949/50, saw the systematic destruction of all forms of Tibetan, especially Buddhist, art and culture as part of Mao's Cultural Revolution and overall policy of 'Sinofication', aimed at eradicating any vestiges of a separate Tibetan identity. The scale of the physical destruction can be gauged by the fact that, of the six thousand temples in existence before the invasion, two decades later only thirteen survived intact. The rest were looted and structurally damaged, and their contents were either destroyed or taken to China, to be melted down, sold on the export market or distributed among public or private collections. One Chinese factory alone is recorded as having melted down over 570 tons (580 tonnes) of looted statues. The Chinese also closed every craft workshop and artistic institution in Tibet (with the exception of those making domestic utensils) and forced the craftsmen to take up alternative employment. In the early 1980s over thirteen thousand images were returned to Tibet, and some restoration work was permitted. It is to be hoped that this represents a genuine change of policy by the new Chinese authorities.

A mass exodus of Tibetan refugees started in the late 1950s and early 1960s, and since then all Tibetan rugs (and other arts and crafts) have been produced by Tibetan exiles. Most escaped across the Himalayas into Nepal, northern India (especially Sikkim and Ladakh) and, to a lesser extent, Bhutan, where, like refugees everywhere, they were faced with the prospect of having to earn a living. Very few of them were carpet-weavers by trade, but rug-making had the distinct advantages of a) requiring little capital investment, b) using readily available materials, c) allowing the refugees to work in small, collective groups, d) not competing with local industries, and e) catering for an existing international market. Consequently, a few rug-making workshops were sponsored (mainly through the United Nations and other aid agencies) in both India and Nepal, and the 'Tibetan' rugs produced in these countries are now more widely known and appreciated than when they were made in Tibet.

Nepalese-Tibetan rugs

Hand-knotted rugs have been made in the Nepalese highlands by indigenous craftsmen for centuries, but these items (known locally as *Raadi, Paakhi* and *Gailaincha*) were almost exclusively woven for personal use, and, in a commercial sense, the Nepalese rug-making industry only began with the introduction of Tibetan refugees. Families, or groups of friends, set up simple wooden looms in their homes, and, as the market for their rugs began to expand, these operations developed into small workshops, often consisting of little more than two or three looms in a cowshed. A few local entrepreneurs recognized the potential, and invested in larger workshops, or manufactories, later establishing contact with major European and North American importers (e.g. Kelati, Eastern Khayam, Rubenir, Amiran and Masterlooms). With the added support of the Nepalese government and international aid agencies, rug-making has developed into Nepal's single most important export industry.

Today there are over 500 workshops employing over 100,000 (mostly female) workers, in addition to the thousands who earn a living in the various support industries, ranging from tourist shops to printing and advertising. There are also in excess of 200 exporters of varying sizes, who between them sell over 1 million square metres (worth more than $70 million) to the West annually; from the mid-1980s both the quantity and foreign earnings have increased steadily each year, making Nepal the fourth- or fifth-largest exporter in the world.

The organization of the Nepalese rug-making industry is a mixture of local private enterprise, multi-national contracting and distribution, and government control. The vast majority of workshops are concentrated in Boudha, Swayambhu, Jawalakhel, Pokhara and a number of other towns and villages, mainly in the Kathmandu valley, as well as in Kathmandu itself. Some are totally independent, and distribute their rugs through small, equally independent, exporters, but the vast majority are contracted, sometimes exclusively, to one of the large Western importers.

The entire rug-making industry is regulated by the Central Corporate Carpet Association, who exercise a high degree of control over pricing, weaving standards and working conditions, as well as acting as a general marketing and promotional body for both local (mainly tourist) and international sales. A crucial role in these areas is also played by the major Western importers, who have an interest in ensuring that the industry maintains both a high standard of quality control and the ability to produce rugs on time, at the right price, and in the designs and colour schemes required for each of their different markets.

In the mid-1980s, there were justifiable criticisms of both the inconsistent quality of Nepalese-Tibetan rugs, and poor business practices (e.g. failure to meet delivery dates, selling already contracted goods, and misrepresenting artificial silk as genuine silk). Fortunately, however, the Nepalese weaving industry has shown a willingness to learn from its mistakes, and, in

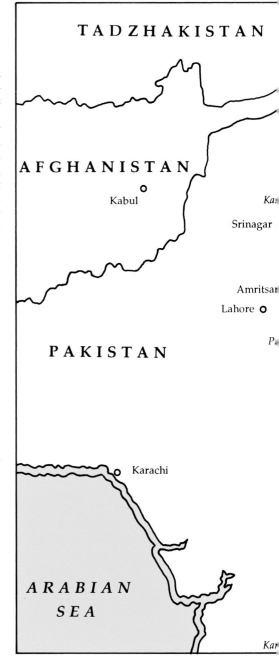

partnership with Western importers, a much higher standard of overall consistency was achieved during the late 1980s and early 1990s.

Nepalese-Tibetan rugs are generally attractive, well made, durable and reasonably priced, but they are not subject to the same standards of consistently applied quality controls as Chinese rugs. Excellent items are produced, but there are others whose aesthetic and technical quality leaves something to be desired. It is therefore important to treat each rug on its own merits, and to examine several before making a final choice – particularly as there is often very little difference in price between good and mediocre rugs.

The vast majority of Nepalese-Tibetan rugs have woollen piles, and are woven in the traditional Tibetan manner (p. 29), using good quality, sometimes hand-spun, wool on cotton foundations, and either synthetic or natural dyes, or sometimes a combination of both. In the very finest items Tibetan wool is used on its own, but most rugs are made with a roughly equal mixture of Tibetan and New Zealand wool. In addition, a small number of silk and artificial silk items are produced. The fineness of the knotting is normally measured in knots per in^2 and the standard commercial quality is approximately 36 per in^2 (i.e. 72-line); although much finer, 100 knots per in^2 (or 120-line), items are also made. Silk rugs normally employ a minimum of 100 knots per in^2.

Designs may be traditionally Tibetan or Westernized versions of Tibetan schemes. Traditional compositions are often copies of old rugs, and include dragon, phoenix, medallion, floral (frequently peony), chessboard, snow leopard and tiger designs (pls. 27–39). Westernized Tibetan schemes are usually based on variations of medallion, geometric and floral themes (pl. 23).

Completely Western designs are also produced, and may be based on established rug schemes (e.g. Aubusson, Art Deco, Art Nouveau) or totally original compositions (pl. 25). Like the Westernized Tibetan schemes, they are frequently produced by designers employed directly by the major importers, such as Kelati, Tufekian and Odegard. In addition, there are a number of 'hybrid' compositions which take elements from other rug-making traditions and merge them with more traditional Tibetan, or, occasionally, Western designs (pl. 27).

The Tibetan rug-producing areas of northern India, Nepal and Bhutan

Colour schemes are usually executed in pastel shades, using a wide range of pigments, particularly blues, violets, greens, and yellow, brown and orange ochres, although brighter, more traditional hues are sometimes employed. Much depends on the washing process, and the degree to which a chemical wash is used to tone down the intensity of the dyes (p. 28). Some larger workshops have their own washing facilities; but most either use one of the independent companies in Kathmandu, or export their rugs unwashed and leave the final finish to the importing companies. The cost of washing in Nepal can be as little as a third of the cost of having the rugs washed abroad. However, the facilities in the West are more sophisticated, and unwashed rugs allow the major importers a degree of flexibility in satisfying any sudden fluctuations in demand from different markets, as well as enabling them to exercise tighter quality control.

Classifying Nepalese-Tibetan rugs is extremely difficult. There are no individual weaving groups, as such; nor are there the same clearly defined ranges, as in China. However, Nepalese-Tibetan production can be broadly divided into what might be best described as 'authentic Tibetan' and 'non-authentic, or Westernized, Nepali-Tibetan' rugs.

Nepali-Tibetan rugs (pls. 23, 25, 27, 34) represent over 95% of the rugs produced in Nepal, and are aimed almost exclusively at the mass furnishing market. They are generally well made, using a mixture of Tibetan and New Zealand wool, employ reliable, colour-fast, synthetic (and occasionally natural) dyes, and are woven in both 36 and 100 knots per in^2 qualities. Silk and artificial silk items are also made. They are usually produced under the auspices, or in conjunction with, the major Western importers, and feature the widest possible range of colours and designs, including some traditional Tibetan schemes, which can usually be distinguished from 'authentic Tibetan' rugs by their more muted, pastel shades. For example, a number of traditional Tiger rugs (p. 116) are now produced which are almost exact copies of 18th- and 19th-century rugs, but they can usually be distinguished from the originals by the lack of intensity in their colours (due to washing) and the way in which the scheme has been 'cleaned' or 'tidied' around the edges, subduing the often primitive exuberance of the earlier versions of the design.

Nepali-Tibetan rugs should therefore be considered as attractive, good quality, reasonably priced furnishing items, rather than as collectable or investment examples of textile art. They are usually marketed simply as Nepali, or Nepali-Tibetan, rugs, but are sometimes referred to as Kangris. However, they may also be sold under the name of almost any Tibetan or Nepalese place or design.

Authentic Tibetan rugs (pls. 28–33, 35–9) constitute only a very small part of contemporary Nepalese production, and are the almost exclusive preserve of a handful of workshops that are endeavouring to keep the authentic traditions of Tibetan weaving alive. As with other Nepalese rugs, Western importers play a vital role, but these items cater for a more specialized market and are normally handled by small, independent companies (such as Alain Rouveure) who have a personal interest in preserving Tibetan culture.

Authentic Tibetan rugs are of exceptional aesthetic and structural integrity, using (wherever possible) only genuine Tibetan wool and natural dyes, and reproducing unmodified contemporary versions of traditional designs. They are not given the usual colour-reducing chemical washes, and consequently their colour schemes possess an intensity that is usually lacking in Nepali-Tibetan rugs. Because of the high quality of their manufacture, and the small number being produced each year, they are more expensive than standard Nepali-Tibetan items, but represent excellent value for money and have the best chance of any contemporary Nepalese-Tibetan rugs of becoming collectable in the future. They are normally marketed simply as Tibetan rugs, or Tibetan rugs made in Nepal, although they may also be sold under the name of the individual workshop, importer or traditional design.

Indian-Tibetan rugs

Tibetan rug-making in India has developed along different, less commercial lines than in Nepal. Indian-Tibetan production is focused around small, widely dispersed pockets of Tibetan craftsmen operating from partially sponsored craft centres, run under the auspices of the Council for Home Affairs (a department of the Tibetan government-in-exile), the Council for Economic Affairs and the Dalai Lama's Charitable Trust for Handicraft Exports.

The first of these craft centres was established in 1949, in the old hill station of Dalhousie (in Himachal Pradesh), under the management of the Indian Co-operative Union, employing around five hundred Tibetan refugees (many with rug-making experience) and serving as a model for similar centres throughout northern India. This is almost identical to the way in which workshops initially developed in Nepal, but, unlike Nepal, the Tibetan weaving centres in India have so far failed to attract either local or foreign commercial interest. Consequently, the entire rug-making operation remains a localized cottage industry which has yet to make any impact on the export market. However, from the late 1970s efforts have been made to promote the industry; a showroom and export centre was established in New Delhi, and shops were opened in Dharamasala (Himachal Pradesh), Bangalore (Karnataka) and Manali (a small village in the Kula valley bordering the Punjab and Himachal Pradesh). In addition, a central wool-buying agency was set up in Amritsar (the Punjab), which now supplies almost all the wool used by the weaving centres, and the Council for Home Affairs established a further marketing unit in New Delhi. Approximately 40% of all Indian-Tibetan rugs are distributed through these central marketing organizations; the rest are sold directly by the workshops themselves.

The weaving centres are spread throughout northern India, mainly in Ladakh, Sikkim, Himachal Pradesh, Arunachal Pradesh and Uttar Pradesh, and there are also small concentrations of workshops around Hunsur in the southern state of Karnataka. These vary in size from small family workshops producing only twenty to thirty rugs each year, to larger workshop/manufactories capable of weaving in excess of twelve hundred items per annum. Currently, there are just over forty weaving centres in India, but their entire production is over fifteen times less than that of Nepal. Many of these centres are family, or extended family, concerns, with women doing most of the weaving, and men undertaking the dyeing, clipping, washing and overall supervision

of production and design. Most of the centres in the Himalayan states close down in the winter, because they cannot afford to heat the workshops, and the entire workforce often migrates south to sell sweaters.

Indian-Tibetan rugs are generally more authentic in character and appearance than those produced in Nepal, but tend to be largely confined to the more 'nomadic' or 'peasant' Tibetan weaving traditions, with very few examples of the more sophisticated, classic designs. Tibetan, Indian and imported wool is used, although the amount of Tibetan wool available has increased in recent years since the Council for Economic Affairs (the 'Paljor') initiated a scheme for buying it directly from Tibetan nomads in Ladakh and other Himalayan border states, and then distributing it to centres throughout the country. There are no standard qualities or grades of Indian-Tibetan rugs, but they are usually around 36 knots per in^2 (72-line) or fewer, and are generally well made, durable (especially those using Tibetan wool) and attractive.

Designs are generally based on old carpets, although some more individualistic variations are produced, and feature a wide range of traditional floral, medallion, animal, bird and religious/philosophical motifs. The more profound Buddhist symbols are rarely used, however, as they are considered too sacred. Colours tend to be rather bright and cheerful, although more tonally harmonious and subdued schemes are also produced.

Categorizing Indian-Tibetan rugs is extremely difficult, despite the existence of of identifiable weaving centres, because of the lack of clearly evolved regional styles. Some workshops, especially those in Dehra Dun (Uttar Pradesh), Bomdila (Arunachal Pradesh), Choglamsar (Ladakh) and Hunsur (Karnataka), have established a reputation for quality and produce items with some distinctive characteristics, but this pattern is not repeated consistently throughout the country. Consequently, it is perhaps more valuable to categorize Indian-Tibetan rugs into the three styles produced by most weaving centres, corresponding to the major markets: Tibetan, Indian and tourist.

Rugs for the Tibetan market are generally very colourful, usually with at least ten or eleven different colours, and employ heavily patterned designs. Distinctive borders are a regular feature, and the brightly articulated scheme is frequently set against a dark blue background (similar to pls. 29, 30). They are bought primarily by Tibetan refugees and people of Tibetan descent, and can be found especially in Dharamasala (the unofficial capital of the exiled Tibetan community).

Rugs for the Indian market also tend to be bright and colourful, but employ harmonious rather than contrasting colour combinations, often with varying shades of the same basic hue. Designs vary, but floral schemes are usually the most popular (similar to pls. 28, 32). Many of these items are made under commission from army officers, clubs and societies, and rich families.

Rugs for the foreign tourist market are generally more pastel in colour with relatively bold, and often simple, designs, featuring distinctive borders. These are normally the most 'nomadic' in character and appearance of all Indian-Tibetan rugs, and are often made with some, if not all, undyed wool. It is quite common to find natural (vegetable) dyes (pl. 37) – although synthetic dyes are also used.

Further information on Tibetan weaving in India can be obtained from H.H. the Dalai Lama's Charitable Trust for Handicraft Exports, 16 Jor Bagh, Lodi Road, New Delhi 10003, India.

Weaving in Ladakh and Sikkim

In addition to the rugs made by refugees, some items are produced by people of Tibetan descent who have occupied these regions for centuries. These rugs are essentially nomadic, featuring very simple geometric designs – they are sometimes even patternless – and frequently woven in a mixture of undyed wool and yak hair. They are produced primarily for personal use, but some may be found for sale in Leh (Ladakh), Gangtok (Sikkim) or other marketing towns.

These items are amongst the most primitive produced anywhere in the world, and rarely find their way into the rest of India, let alone the West. However, they possess a distinctive, rough-hewn charm, and anything woven as a buffer against the Himalayan winter should have little problem withstanding domestic use.

Bhutanese rugs

Very little is known about Bhutanese rug-making because the country was more or less closed to foreigners until the early 1980s; even today, only a limited number of tourists are permitted each year. However, Bhutan has a sizeable population of both native Tibetans and recent refugees, and a small number of essentially Tibetan rugs are produced. The majority are brightly coloured and feature a number of traditional designs, especially dragons (not surprisingly, as Bhutan is known locally as the 'Thunder Dragon Kingdom'). They are roughly equivalent in quality to the Nepalese-Tibetan 36 knots per in^2 (72-line) grade. As yet, they are not exported in any numbers, and usually only find their way to the West through visitors who have purchased them in Thimphu or one of the other major towns.

Index